Human Collaboration at Work

Human Collaboration at Work delves into the dynamics of collaboration between two individuals, examining both the challenges and potential in creative relationships and offering a useful resource for all those working with others. The two-person relationship is one of the key building blocks in our understanding of relationships in organizations yet is largely understudied in the literature.

This book brings the dyadic relationship to the fore and offers support for those engaging in collaborative relationships in the workplace and beyond. The author reframes challenges as opportunities for partners to leverage their differences and overcome potential conflicts. Through this lens, he provides a nuanced understanding of the interpersonal and contextual factors that influence collaboration.

Supported by compelling real-life examples, including the author's own long-term working relationship with a colleague, this book is an essential guide for those in leadership roles, managers, consultants, and academics alike – anyone seeking to enhance their collaborative relationships in professional settings.

David N. Berg is an organizational psychologist with 15 years of experience teaching at the Yale School of Management, USA. He is currently Clinical Professor of Psychiatry at the Yale School of Medicine, where he teaches, supervises, and consults in the area of organizational behavior with students, medical residents, faculty, and administration.

Human Collaboration at Work

Challenge and Potential in Creative Relationships

David N. Berg

Routledge
Taylor & Francis Group
NEW YORK AND LONDON

Designed cover image: Getty Images @melitas

First published 2025
by Routledge
605 Third Avenue, New York, NY 10158

and by Routledge
4 Park Square, Milton Park, Abingdon, Oxon, OX14 4RN

Routledge is an imprint of the Taylor & Francis Group, an informa business

ISBN: 9781032701912 (hbk)
ISBN: 9781032701882 (pbk)
ISBN: 9781032701998 (ebk)

DOI: 10.4324/9781032701998

Typeset in Sabon
by codeMantra

Dedicated to Rachel and Sophia
whose existence, the fruit of a collaboration,
is both a miracle and a joy.

Contents

Preface

For some reason, undoubtedly rooted in my early life, I have been curious about what is not talked about but what I know to be real. When I was ten my parents divorced. I was never told, perhaps appropriately, the story behind that event. I could feel the reality of a relationship that often seemed joyless and tense, but no one spoke about it. In hindsight, not hearing the whole story may have made my childhood suffering worse. It spared me nothing and deprived me of some attempt at understanding, especially since in 1959 mine was the only "broken" home in my grade.

In graduate school, my attempts to help people in organizations to align their values with their behavior often resulted in failure. Everyone I talked to about these failed attempts, other graduate students as well as professors young and old, not only commiserated but offered their own accounts of failure. When a student colleague of mine and I searched the literature in our field, we found nothing published. The only "findings" published in professional journals were successes. Although everyone had encountered failure, no one wrote about it. No one was willing to go on the record about what all of us knew to be real. Phil Mirvis and I compiled a book of case studies of failures and the learnings they spawned. Many in our field preferred not to contribute, fearing their names would be forever linked to failure.

Later, I felt drawn to what struck me as an incomplete treatment of conflict in groups. Too often conflict was either problematic (to be avoided in a cohesive group) or something to be gotten through (a stage or phase on the way to high performance). "Constructive" conflict was a part of the story, but even it carried more than a whiff of pathology. I had never been part of a productive group (of friends, co-workers, classmates) that had not included multiple and often intense conflicts. Something was missing in the conventional stories about groups and conflict. Kenwyn Smith and I wrote a book about the *normal* tensions and conflicts in groups. We tried to wrestle with the relatively undiscussed question of why conflict was such a regular and recurring feature of group life.

At a time when leadership was all the rage, when organizations would actually espouse the need for "leaders" not "followers," when advertisements used slogans like "lead, follow or get out of the way" or "some lead, others follow," and when every executive development course had to have the word "leadership" in its title, I became curious about what was being ignored in this over-the-top (sic) emphasis on leadership. So, I began to examine the relationship between leadership and followership.

I notice a few patterns in this brief personal academic history. Clearly, I am curious about what is not talked about. Success and failure, harmony and conflict, leadership and followership are all aspects of every human's experience. But one of these paired experiences gets a lot more attention than the other. I believed, and still believe, that this lopsided attention distorts our understanding of human endeavors and even more importantly, hampers our ability to thrive in the various relationships that make up human existence. This book is about the aspects of two-person collaboration that are not often discussed.

My aspiration for this book is that it becomes a conversation between words on a page and the reader, a living, breathing human being. Toward that end, I have made a few choices about pronouns. I often write in the first person. When the thoughts, observations, concepts, or stories are mine, writing in the first person emphasizes my personal connection and, I hope, invites you to explore your personal reactions to them. This is an attempt to invite you to reflect on your experience, considering how and why it is similar or different from mine. I hope this choice helps create a relationship between my thoughts and yours. I also use the pronoun "we" quite a lot, as in "we will return to this example later." Here again, my choice of pronoun is an invitation to join me in examining the ideas in this book. Though we are not sitting in living room discussing collaboration, I prefer evoking that setting to a classroom lecture or a bookstore reading. I would like reading this book to feel as much like a discussion as possible. We'll see if the choice of pronoun helps. Finally, I have struggled with the gendered nature of our third-person pronouns. When I am writing about actual people, alive or dead, I will use the pronouns they used, usually he/she and him/her. In some cases, I will use "they" to refer to a single individual. I have chosen to do this for two reasons. The first is that gendered pronouns are not interchangeable. Alternating he and she, for example, can change the meaning of a sentence. To write "She broke down in tears" is not the equivalent of writing "He broke down in tears." Whenever possible I have tried to think carefully about my choice of singular pronoun. The other reason for using "they" to refer to a single person is because, like Whitman, I believe we contain multitudes. Each time I use "they" I hope you will think that the individual I am writing about can and does include a variety of identities, identities that should not be reduced or constrained by the pronoun I use.

Gratitude

In the creation of a book about collaboration, it should not be surprising that I believe strongly that a great many relationships contributed to what follows. It is a pleasure to express my gratitude to some of them. My apologies to those I have omitted unintentionally. All who follow, as well as those who spoke to me in confidence and on the record, have donated their wisdom and experience to this project, some more directly than others, but all in ways that continue to touch me deeply. I am grateful for your contributions.

Catherine Durnell Crampton, now a distinguished emerita professor, was once a research assistant for me. Our project, in the late 1980s, was a collaboration. When I began the preparation for this book, I retrieved my notes from that initial foray into the topic. The work that Catherine had done literally stunned me. Her research was thorough, but it was her insight and thoughtfulness that struck me the most. After more than 30 years, the quality of her contribution to this work remains solid and deep. Ours was a genuine, albeit brief, collaboration on collaboration. I am grateful that she was present and engaged at the beginning of this journey.

There were formative academic collaborations that preceded my work with Catherine. My undergraduate roommate, Ernest S. Robson III, gave me a first taste of two people creating something for a class at Yale. We were given a failing grade, but I remember the joy of the experience. Many thanks to Ernie. Phil Mirvis was my first professional writing partner and collaborator. We were different in many ways (how could it be otherwise), but Phil was kind, patient, creative, and great fun. Cortlandt Cammann, a lifelong friend, was a research collaborator extraordinaire. His interest in learning *with* as opposed to teaching *to* cemented a professional relationship in which I felt loved as well as intellectually stimulated.

Greg Shea offered to collaborate on a project that connected us, a former graduate student and a young professor, when Greg went to work in a manufacturing company, and I remained at a university. I am grateful for that early lesson in complementarity, complete with expected and unexpected challenges. Nancy Connito was a partner on the Bethany School Board, a collaboration that taught me, in a very personal way, about relationships embedded in a social and political environment. She was often a life preserver in a choppy sea. In my early years at Yale, a place in which I have always felt moderately uncomfortable, Jim Ponet found me and introduced me to the pleasures of *havruta*, the study of the Talmud done in pairs. He was my partner and collaborator; he will always be my teacher and my friend. Marshall Edelson, a co-author, and co-teacher dragged me into our collaboration, and much as I complained about the process, I will be forever grateful to Marshall for introducing me to a world that spawned many wonderful and meaningful collaborations. Jessica Moldovan and Ali Weiner, generations later, each held on to our relationship long after the formal classroom context in which we met had ended. The holding on was mutual, but the commitment is deeply appreciated. Bill Kahn and I adopted each other when he was a graduate student, and I was an assistant professor. I have long appreciated the depth of his psychological curiosity. We play together in ways that are enjoyable, freeing, and stimulating. Thank you, Bill. Alex Simon is a recent addition to the collaborators who have taught me about collaboration. I often did not like the lessons I found myself learning when we taught together, but every one was important and the conflict that regularly emerged always came from a place of love.

Betsy Bradley has been a colleague and co-creator for almost 20 years. I am grateful to Betsy for her honesty and integrity both within our relationship and when facing an outside world that is complex and challenging, especially when it comes to honesty and integrity. Lauren Taylor is quite simply a gift that keeps on giving. Filled with ideas she contributed in substantive ways to the ideas in this book with her abiding interest, timely suggestions, and intellectual rigor. I am grateful that fate put Allison Ponce in my path over a decade ago. She has become a full collaborator in an educational realm that I chose to inhabit alone for far too long. Being with her in that professional world has been a joy. Kristina Talbert-Slagle brought science into my life after I ran from it in eighth grade. It was thrilling. But more than that we became collaborators in many areas and across many differences in expertise and background. That she is from Kentucky, and I am from New Jersey may capture it all. I treasure her. Valentina Greco has enriched the last decade of my life in more ways than I can count or recount. Her willingness and ability to look across disciplines, cultures, and identities to make deep and creative connections has been an inspiration to me. She regularly expresses her love to those she cares about, and I am grateful to be in that group.

There are a few people who have been with me on this journey for 50 years or more. Howard Dean did not flinch in the face of my adolescent intensity, and we have been friends ever since. Late in life we created and taught a course together, a collaboration that illustrates many of the themes in this book. It is also a collaboration that renewed a relationship for which I am grateful. Leroy Wells, Jr. was an early collaborator, a man with deep insight into interpersonal and intergroup relations who, as a younger peer, shaped my professional identity in profound ways. I miss him terribly. Our collaborations were cut short by his untimely death, but his heart and mind are always with me. Clayton Alderfer was the person whose integrity and commitment beckoned me into the profession I have now long cherished. He placed relationships at the center of his understanding of organizations and society. He supported me through every struggle and accomplishment, both personal and professional, throughout my adult life. He was a mentor in the deepest way that Dan Levinson used the term. We were both only children. In Alderfer, I found an older brother who became a colleague, collaborator, and friend. He was always (actuarially) going to leave this world before me, but I wish it hadn't been so soon. He was the source.

Kenwyn K. Smith has been, and continues to be, the collaboration of a lifetime. We met in graduate school and for over 50 years we have been in each other's lives. My experience of and reflections on our relationship are the foundation of this book, but more importantly, they are one of the core foundations of my adult life. My feelings about Smith transcend simple gratitude for what he has contributed to my life. I am grateful for his presence in my life and for the mysterious forces in the universe that brought us together.

Finally, I want to express my gratitude for my wife, Robin Golden, who has lived through every element of collaboration that is detailed in this book. In addition to sharing the collaborative joys and struggles of parenthood, Robin read the entire manuscript and gave invaluable feedback with love and tenderness. She is both a partner and a collaborator in many, many ways. I am grateful for them all.

David Berg, *New Haven, Connecticut*

Chapter 1

Introduction

This is a book about human collaboration, the relationship between two people that creates something neither could have created alone, a creation born of their differences and nurtured in the connection between them. Collaboration goes beyond the heartfelt appreciation that we have for the contributions of others to our own accomplishments. Collaboration describes creativity that comes not from the mind of one person but from the relationship between them. The Gilbert and Sullivan collaboration that spawned numerous light operas of immense popularity across decades brought together an above-average playwright with a competent composer to create magical musical theater. John Lennon and Paul McCartney were extremely talented as individuals, but together their music was extraordinary in scope and influence. Bundini Brown was an itinerant corner man for professional boxers and Mohammad Ali was a supreme fighter, but together many have credited them with laying the foundation for hip-hop and rap music.[1] Emily Doudna and Emmanuelle Charpentier were each making significant contributions to their individual biological subdisciplines, but together they invented a process that changed genetics forever.

More specifically, this is a book about two-person collaborations. Focusing on a two-person collaboration allows us to examine the essential nature of the collaborative relationship without the added complexity of groups or teams. The question of who speaks, when and why, can be a challenging one when observing two people trying to create a mission statement. Their personalities and backgrounds, the cultural context in which they find themselves, the topic of conversation, and the "agendas" that each may bring to the discussion all may bear on the simple issue of participation. Now consider these same questions with five or six people in a meeting devoted to the same purpose. What needs to be observed, no less interpreted and understood, is exponentially greater. The two-person relationship reveals dynamics that are also at work in a larger group, but we may have trouble seeing them amidst the overwhelming complexity of the group setting.

DOI: 10.4324/9781032701998-1

Focusing on the two-person relationship also means there is less chance that these essential dynamics will be submerged or displaced onto others. If I am feeling some tension in my relationship with team member Sally, I can avoid sitting next to her and focus my comments on Rashid with whom, at the moment, I am not feeling any tension. Why did I move? Was it something about Sally, Rashid, my relationship to one or the other, or just a random choice (if you believe in random choices)? In a two-person collaboration, if I am feeling some tension with Jesse, it will play itself out more directly as avoidance, awkwardness, or confrontation. Much easier to observe and examine.

There is something lost in the choice to focus on two-person collaborations as well. Many collaborations that appear to involve two people involve many others. A focus on two-person collaborations contributes to the myth that individuals – albeit two in this case – are the essential source of creativity. When we look more deeply into these relationships, the contributions of others are quickly revealed. The collaboration of Watson and Crick, the "discoverers" of the structure of DNA, is a case in point. Many people worked in their labs and many labs were working on the same problem at the same time! Focusing on the two-person relationship puts the group dynamics of collaboration in the background. For this book, I am choosing simplicity (at the risk of oversimplifying) in the service of shedding light on unexamined dynamics in these important two-person relationships.

Why Write a Book on Collaboration?

The collaborative process, by its very nature, both leverages and strains relationships. My longest-running collaboration, with Kenwyn Smith, an Aussie whom I met in graduate school, has produced two books, several academic papers, numerous teaching endeavors, and a deep friendship. The books, papers, and courses are the creative output of our decades-long work together. And it is also true that at times I felt erased or eclipsed by Smith's notoriety or reputation. I periodically wondered about my own individual "productivity." It fused me, professionally, with my dear colleague forever, a reality that, to this day, is a source of both deep satisfaction and periodic dismay. But these emotions were not what I had anticipated. Yes, there were many times when the collaboration was uplifting and productive. But there were also times when I felt competitive, envious, second-fiddle, invisible, and insecure. I had chosen this collaboration. I respected and came to love Smith. Where were these other feelings coming from? Was it normal to have such feelings or was there something wrong with me or with us?

We are taught very little about the benefits and challenges of collaborative relationships. The adage of "no pain, no gain" tells us that success requires hard work. But who is doing this work is left unspecified. People often talk generally about the positive aspects of "working together," but the struggles of working with another person, which this book will show are both essential and ubiquitous, receive much less attention. When we are invited to collaborate with someone, for example, what do we think, how do we feel? A friend proposes we create a speech together to deliver at another friend's wedding or a co-worker from another department suggests we work together to create a better workflow process. Depending upon who initiates the collaborative invitation (the wedding speech friend), the joy and possibilities spring to mind, but not the inevitable challenges. Other times (the cross-department invitation) the concerns come first, and the possibilities seem remote. Most often, however, collaboration evokes the promise of something new and exciting. When an organization announces a merger with another organization, for example, the press release always touts the advantages of the new relationship even as the members of both organizations realize that making a merger work will be extremely difficult. This is the case with every collaboration. We know in our bones that there is both promise and challenge in working creatively with others. We talk about the promise, we hope the challenges will not materialize. When they do, as they inevitably will, we are not prepared.

Remember being assigned to work with a group in high school or college to write a joint paper or produce a joint project? Four people were assigned to write a paper together with one final grade for all. The assigning teacher may have simply wanted to reduce his paper reading and grading time. But it is also possible that she imagined the paper would be more creative if written from the interchange between four students with different ideas, perspectives, writing styles, and insights. How much did our teachers prepare students for this group collaboration? For many of us, the experience was excruciating (except perhaps for the one person who hardly lifted a finger and got the same grade). Why didn't anyone tell us about the struggles and prepare us for them? What we learned was to avoid classes with a group paper. We may even have learned to avoid "collaborations" altogether. We certainly did not learn anything about collaborations that would help us manage their creative potential.

Why don't merging organizations include a description of the hard work ahead or the risks involved when they announce a merger? Why don't high school teachers provide instruction about working in groups, seemingly preferring to let us struggle through it on our own? Why do we avoid telling the whole story about collaborations? Why do we not prepare ourselves and others for the good and the bad, the exhilarations and the tensions, the coming together and the falling apart?

Perhaps we avoid telling the full story about collaborative relationships for the same reason that we, like the wedding officiant who hints at the universally acknowledged fact that marriages take "work," are loathe to dwell on the difficulties that are part of any meaningful collaboration. Perhaps not confronting or being confronted with the arduous reality of a collaborative relationship allows us to undertake the difficult and important work of creating something with someone else. Knowing the full story will come with time as will the decisions to tackle the challenges of collaboration. But the first step in a creative relationship is not the moment to bring up such issues. Not only would such a full story be a downer, but it might dissuade people from entering these relationships in the first place.

Or perhaps we don't tell the whole story because to include struggle and separation in the story of collaboration would be to include the possibility of personal failure and dysfunction in that story. Rather than reframe the role of struggle and separation in the story of collaboration, we rewrite the story to leave out these parts perhaps because we believe these "negative" aspects of collaboration reveal something inadequate about *us* rather than something important about the *collaborative experience more generally*. For example, the way many of us describe our freshman year in college leaves out the loneliness, insecurity, and stress because including the whole story might reflect poorly on the storyteller. But the omission obscures the near universal reality that freshman year can be a struggle.

This book is written for people who are interested in the whole story. Knowing the whole story enables us to sustain collaborative relationships. Reframing collaboration to include struggle and separation better equips us to deal with these challenges without attributing them to our personal failings. Absent the full story, those of us engaged in a collaboration can feel confused and alone when the part of the story we never heard becomes a reality. This confusion and isolation can undermine our ability to manage these rough patches in collaborative work. If, for example, you were never told (in ways that you believed) that wanting alone time from your chosen life partner was normal, you might feel guilty or unfaithful when these feelings emerge. You might try to talk yourself out of the feelings and you certainly might hide them from your partner. Denying or hiding these feelings makes it hard to find out if your partner has similar feelings. It also makes it nearly impossible to address them, to give each partner time and permission to be alone.

Telling the whole story also inoculates us against the impact of these challenges.[2] Much like a vaccine, giving us a dose of those aspects of collaboration that might stress the relationship provides us with the tools to address (and survive) these stresses. The whole story also provides us with "anticipatory socialization,"[3] it prepares us for what is to come so that we are not surprised or unprepared for what the collaboration demands of us. In 1973, the Ford Motor Company was confronted with a massive turnover on the assembly line. It appeared increases in wages could not stem this tide and the retraining costs for replacing every person who left the line were huge. Ultimately, instead of recruiting employees to the assembly line with enticements about pay and benefits, the company produced a film titled "Don't Paint it Like Disneyland," one of the first efforts at a realistic job preview.[4] The company found that telling the whole story reduced the number of people who applied for a job on the assembly line, but also dramatically reduced the turnover of those who did apply. Telling a fuller story about the work of collaboration could have similar effects.[5]

Even when we peel back the layers of highly visible collaborations, how much do we learn about them? What happened to Lennon and McCartney? Did Yoko Ono really cause the break? Or did that storyline make it more difficult to examine how Lennon and McCartney's relationship evolved and what role Yoko Ono played in that evolution? What was married life like for scientists Pierre and Marie Curie? What is it like for any couple who share a professional and personal relationship? Surely the creative comedy of Abbot and Costello was neither as effortless nor as smooth as the final performances suggest. Were they ever estranged during their decades-long career together?[6] If Gilbert and Sullivan wrote light opera simply for the money, what was that collaboration like? How did they split the money? We will dig more deeply into the written accounts of some of these relationships to gain more insight into collaboration. And if we also turn our attention, curious and open, to our own collaborations we might expand our understanding with what we already know in our bones.

I believe we have long understood the challenging side of collaboration even if we do not often include it in our wedding toasts or corporate announcements. Like the DNA in our cells that tells the story of human evolution, language carries with it the complex emotional reality of human experience. The word collaboration is a case in point. Ultimately, the Latin root of the word tells us that working together involves a process that does indeed include falling apart or collapsing. For those of us who have been involved in a collaboration, this description captures something right about creative work that is done with someone else. It is exhausting and exhilarating. Co-working is a complex emotional and physical undertaking. What exactly is this process and why is falling apart an aspect of the word and the experience? Might we gain something from returning the word to its roots, from giving the experience a more complete examination? This book is devoted to answering these questions.

For Whom Is This Book Written?

This book is written for people who are in collaborative relationships, are reflecting on a collaborative relationship that has ended, or are considering getting involved in a collaboration. There is a saying that "the map is not the terrain." The mesa does not soar in front of you and the valleys do not slope gradually to the river no matter what the topographic elevations indicate. The streams do not burble nor do the lakes glisten though they appear blue with wavy lines on the page. And the tiny town, consisting of a single crossroads in rural Texas has little charm when reduced to a printed name at the intersection of column B and row 7. Reading a map does not feel like driving a road or trekking cross-country.

But a map isn't worthless. This book is part map, part field guide, part owner's manual, and part travelogue. And while none of these is a substitute for the experience of hiking, foraging, troubleshooting, or traveling, many of our experiences are enhanced or even made possible by having one or more of these resources with us as we encounter the terrain of life. Maps can tell us what to expect ahead or where to look for water pleasures. A field guide can help us spot and identify the naturally occurring fauna and flora along our trail. The owner's manual takes up space in a drawer or trunk until something breaks down, doesn't work, or makes a worrisome noise. Then it becomes invaluable. And a travelogue, if well done, enhances the joy of travel by helping us find and appreciate the places we visit. This book is intended to be a companion volume to the experience of collaboration in the hopes that it will help the reader survive and thrive in these relationships.

Structure

The chapters ahead lay out and flesh out the dynamics of a two-person collaborative relationship. They examine what brings people together and what pushes them apart. Throughout these chapters we will visit and revisit current and historical collaborations that illustrate these dynamics. Some will be well known because they are in the public eye and have been documented by others. Some will come from private conversations I have had with less well-known collaborators. Some will be personal, collaborations in which I am one of the collaborators.

Chapter 2: Collaboration Defined

This chapter presents a formal definition of human collaboration: creative connection across differences. It will explore the role of divergent thinking in individual creativity and apply that same reasoning to the role of divergence or diversity in the relationship between two people engaged in a creative activity together. It will invite the reader to actively engage the ideas in this book by referring to collaborative relationships in their own lives; personal, professional, or recreational. Finally, it compares collaboration with other descriptions of relationships at work such as cooperation and competition.

Chapter 3: Creativity

This chapter examines the core characteristic of collaboration as we have defined it: a creative product born of a relationship. How do we "normally" think about creativity? What does a creative *relationship* mean considering traditional definitions of creativity? If creativity involves producing something new or novel, who decides what's new or novel? This chapter will move us from an individual conception of creativity to a relational definition while answering these questions.

Chapter 4: Difference

The differences between the two people involved in a collaboration are what make it work. These same differences can interrupt and even imperil the work. Some dimensions of difference appear to be simply individual – personality, approach, style. Most often, however, collaboration also occurs across differences that involve where we come from, how we were educated or trained, our experiences, or our position in various of life's hierarchies. This chapter describes the many dimensions of difference that fuel collaboration work.

Chapter 5: Connection

This chapter seeks to answer the question: What kind of relationship nurtures a creative process that involves people who are significantly different from each other? I describe what is required of the collaborators, two people who choose to work across their differences. What are the characteristics of the relationship itself? What are the challenges and possibilities that arise when differences rather than similarities are the foundation of a working relationship?

Chapter 6: Falling Together

How do collaborative relationships begin? Some are formed out of necessity (Gilbert and Sullivan), some because of opportunity (Doudna and Charpentier), some to earn a living (Ike and Tina Turner), and some are an expression of the pre-existing relationship itself (Berg and Smith). Collaborations are intimate affairs, so intimate that collaborations often spawn gossip about romance between the collaborators. They often fall together the way couples fall in love, deliciously aware of the possibilities, mostly oblivious to any indication of a bumpy ride.

Chapter 7: Driven Apart

The differences that fuel collaboration can evolve to drive apart a collaborative relationship. This chapter examines the ways this happens. In some cases, the differences become irritating and divisive. For example, tensions over credit and acknowledgment create wrenching conflict. In other cases, the identity of the collaboration erases the identity of each individual. The psychological and interpersonal forces that drive a collaboration apart paradoxically enable necessary re-individuation, but they are not usually seen this way. Instead, these tensions are described as driven by egos, insecurities, or jealous interlopers.

Chapter 8: Pulled Apart

This chapter describes the way collaborations are pulled apart from the outside. In an individualistic society, like the United States, there exists a deep investment in determining which *individual* is driving the collaborative relationship. We have a hard time locating creativity in a relationship rather than in an individual. It's as if we do not have a place in the cultural file cabinet for anything other than folders with individual names on them. The result is a relentless effort to pull apart creative relationships. Collaborations are also pulled apart by the "groups" to which each of the individuals belongs.

Chapter 9: Staying In

This chapter discusses approaches to handling the forces that drive collaborations apart, among them the collaborators' insecurities and limitations. The goal of the suggestions in both Chapters 9 and 10 is to help the reader navigate the normal and necessary ebb and flow between being *in* the collaborative entity for the creative process to occur and being *out* of it to re-source the individual contributions that make creativity possible.

Chapter 10: Getting Out, Being Apart

There are times in a collaborative relationship when one or the other person needs to get out. This is both normal and often necessary not only for the individuals but also for the collaboration. The desire to get out is rarely discussed in measured terms within the relationship. Arguments and betrayals speak to a desire to get out of the relationship but also to the feeling of being stuck such that some dramatic breach is required. Paradoxically separation does not always threaten collaboration, it often renews the relationship. How to manage separation is the focus of this chapter.

Chapter 11: Conclusion

The conclusion reiterates the central themes of this book: the definition of collaboration, the importance of difference in the creative relationship, the stresses on the individuals caused by *both* their differences and their increasingly fused identities, the normalcy of periodic episodes of falling apart, and the various approaches to managing the challenges of a collaborative relationship. The conclusion also closes the loop on my own experience with collaboration as I indulge in unpacking (a bit) the reason this book, on intimate, creative relationships, was written alone.

Endnotes

1 Joshua Wolf Shenk, *Powers of Two: Finding the Essence of Innovation in Creative Pairs* (Boston: Eamon Dolan/Houghton Mifflin Harcourt, 2014), p. 3.
2 William J. McGuire, 'The Effectiveness of Persuasive Inoculation,' *Journal of Abnormal and Social Psychology* 62, no. 2 (1961). 327–335.
3 Robert K. Merton, *Social Theory and Social Structure*, enlarged edition (New York: Free Press, 1968), p. 6.
4 Daniel R. Ilgen and Phillip W. Dogoni, 'A Review of Realistic Job Previews,' *Personnel Psychology* 34, no. 4 (1981): 579–594.
5 Patricia G. Roth and Philip L. Roth, 'Reduce Turnover with Realistic Job Previews,' *The CPA Journal* 65, no. 9 (September 1995): 64–68.
6 Bob Thomas, *Bud and Lou: The Abbott and Costello Story* (New York: Putnam, 1977), p. 7.

Chapter 2

Collaboration Defined

The purpose of this chapter is to develop a working definition of collaboration. This definition will guide our examination of the collaborative relationship. We will examine the constituent elements of the definition to better understand the potential as well as the challenges inherent in two-person collaboration. We will also compare collaboration with similar words used to describe working relationships, cooperation, competition, and coordination to understand both the experiential as well as the conceptual similarities and differences among terms. When we move to unpack the dynamics of collaboration, we will have a clear and concise description of the phenomenon.

The focus of this chapter is heavily linguistic. I have made this choice because my observation is that words, especially when we pay attention to their evolution over time, carry the emotional and experiential complexity of the human activity they define. The more a word can capture the full experience of its subject, the more meaningful its semantic contribution. When I say something is "interesting," I may not be conveying much information about the thing or the event. Today, the word "interesting" is often used to obscure any real feeling or judgment precisely because it signals so little to the listener. Other words convey a strong sense of an action or feeling. A single word or phrase can evoke an entire scene and the emotions associated with it. The English word "gobsmacking" is an example. The word means "astonishing," and its meaning is hard to confuse or miss. Just saying the word often evokes the emotion of being astonished. Words, within a language, can provide us with clues about how humans have struggled to include in a linguistic symbol, the complexity of a lived experience. There is often a lot packed into a single word to convey this complexity.

It is also my observation that certain words lose or shed aspects of the human experience they originally intended to convey. In some cases, this seems to happen because the "thing" itself changed. For example, the word "taboo" seems to have lost some of its emotional power as "forbidden"

DOI: 10.4324/9781032701998-2

actions lose their connection to religion and morality. Taboo behaviors now more likely refer to actions outside the norm rather than violations of moral strictures. (Think of the difference between a "fashion taboo" and an "incest taboo.") For much of human history the word "taboo" would not have appeared alongside the word "fashion," but times change and so do the meanings and emotional power of words. There are cases of the reverse, when words have added meaning to convey these same cultural changes. To stay with the theme of forbidden activities, the word "wicked" once meant, simply, evil. Today the word "wicked" has added complexity as the culture incorporates the sometimes-invigorating feeling associated with violating norms or stretching boundaries. "Wicked good" is no longer an oxymoron.

In other cases, the emotional complexity of a word, or more accurately, the emotional complexity of the human phenomenon being conveyed by a word, is too hard to contain and the word evolves to convey a simpler, "de-complexified," partial description of the experience. For example, the word "awful" (full of awe) now connotes something terrible. The concert was awful. The baby had an awful night. What an awful experience. Linguistically, the word "awful" once described the experience of being in the presence of power, raw and mighty. That experience was complex. It was not simply a fearful reaction, though being in the presence of raw power – be it natural (e.g., hurricane) or human (e.g., aerial bombardment) or superhuman (e.g., God) – certainly can arouse fear. It is also an experience that can include wonder, humility, and respect. When a word sheds one part of its meaning as a concession to the difficulty human beings have in holding on to emotional complexity, something is lost: the capacity of the word to express the full lived experience of the phenomenon. Over time, the word itself contributes to an incomplete, and even distorted, understanding of the experience. At another level, the word no longer aligns with our actual experience. It can become, like the word "interesting," a simplified linguistic placeholder for a complex emotional experience. It is my contention that this is what has happened to the word collaboration. To examine this contention, we will look at the relationship between collaboration and other words describing working relationships.

Cooperation

We begin with cooperation, the word, and the experience. Cooperation derives from the Latin word opus which means work. The term magnum opus is most often used to describe an individual's great work. Adding "co-" to the root gives us "to work with" as a definition of cooperation. In the social sciences, cooperation has been a rich topic of study.[1] At the heart of game theory[2] are questions of cooperation. Under what conditions do two people work together? What influences the likelihood that people will cooperate? And at the heart of the study of cooperation is the analysis of the decisions individuals make to maximize their personal benefit when the choices (or actions) of others are involved. In cooperative "games" people communicate with each other to find their shared interests and then work together to attain those shared interests. The alignment of shared interests is central to the definition of cooperation. Without shared interests, the incentive to work together is likely to disappear, transforming into exploitation.

Non-cooperative games are those situations in which the people involved cannot communicate with each other.[3] This makes finding shared interests very difficult. In non-cooperative games working together is possible but highly unlikely given the restrictions on communication. The Prisoner's Dilemma is the classic illustration of a non-cooperative game, but one that also defines cooperation. Two thieves are taken to separate jail cells. Since the authorities do not have enough evidence to convict either one, they try to pressure each thief to testify against the other with the following "deal." If Thief A implicates Thief B, Thief A goes free, and Thief B goes to jail for three years. If Thief B implicates Thief A, Thief B goes free, and Thief A goes to jail for three years. If both thieves implicate each other, both go to jail for two years. If both thieves refuse to implicate each other, they each serve one year. The fact that the two thieves are isolated from each other makes the point that the cooperative "solution," the choice that limits the jail time for both, is difficult to find because the risk of staying silent is great and the two thieves cannot talk with each other.

The "game" changes dramatically if the two thieves are allowed to communicate. The communication creates the opportunity to assess the various outcomes and agree on a mutually beneficial course of action. But circumstances, both current and historical, often make this communication, the iterative back and forth that allows two people to identify their shared interests, difficult. Buyers in the Roman marketplace were instructed to beware of Sellers (*caveat emptor*), making the negotiation a process of defending oneself from exploitation rather than discovering a price that meets the needs of both parties. Like the two thieves, the self-interests of both Buyer and Seller in the absence of a mechanism for trustworthy communication and accountability make cooperation unlikely. We can think of cooperation as a description of a process of communication that includes identifying shared interests, making a plan, executing a plan, and additionally, agreeing on enforceable consequences if someone reneges on the plan.

It will come as no surprise that so-called cooperative games are not as interesting to mathematical game theorists as non-cooperative games. The world seems full of missed opportunities for individuals, or groups, or nations to work together because the circumstances prohibit or persistently distort the communication process. Who reveals a strategy to an adversary? But some social scientists have found the domain of cooperative games important and fascinating, since the world is also full of individuals and groups who want to work together but cannot overcome the obstacles to communication, planning, and trust. The fields of negotiation and conflict resolution explore these obstacles, seeking to make it easier for those who wish to cooperate to do so.[4,5]

Competition

The word competition derives from the Latin *petere* which means to try to obtain or to seek. Again, when we add the prefix "com" meaning "with," the word becomes competition, to seek or strive together with another. Clearly something has been lost in the connotation of competition today. The common meaning we give to competition is to strive *against* rather than to strive *with*. Competing is a striving to defeat an opponent or an adversary. It is an activity, in its essence, designed to distinguish between the best and the second best. Competition is the process by which we test two people (or products or ideas) against each other. We are striving against the other to obtain the prize, the sale, the patent, the discovery, the fame, or the recognition. Where is the presence of "striving together with another" in our usage of the word competition?

Upon further reflection, the "with" is evident. In the most basic sense, without the other there is no competition, no striving at all. The presence and action of the other creates the competition. The other pushes us, challenges us, and makes possible the test of our skills and talents. Arriving at a tennis court without an opponent is the absence of competition. Even when "competing with ourselves," our previous standard, our figurative other self, is the competition. Without setting that standard, without establishing some "other" record or accomplishment, competition would not be possible. The other must show up or be present in the "field of play" whether that field is a literal patch of ground or a professional arena. Practice is something we do with ourselves. Competition is something we do with others. We may prepare for competition with others by competing with ourselves, but this involves making the self temporarily an "other." When we compete with a teammate for a starting spot on the team, that competition transforms two people who are working together, cooperating in the service of shared interests, into two people who are competing, striving together to determine who will best represent the team at a particular position.

This last example suggests that cooperation and competition are almost always found together. Both are activities we do together. We sometimes lose sight of the cooperative nature of competition, but the word itself puts this reality front and center. *Com-petere*. Striving together. In ancient times human hunting or human shelter construction required cooperation. Alone, humans were limited in what they could accomplish and thus limited in their ability to survive. But the problem confronting a group (or in our case a pair) of people who want to cooperate is how to allocate themselves to the task. If, in hunting the wooly mammoth, we randomly allocate people to the tasks of tracking, corralling, spearing, skinning, preserving, and sewing, the odds are that we are doing most of these tasks sub-optimally. Instead, we invented tournaments, competitions that identified those among us who were best at certain tasks so that they could be assigned to work that would best serve our shared interests (food, shelter, and clothing in the case of the mammoth hunt). The better the competition, the better the allocation of human resources.

One further note about competition that will inform our discussion of collaboration. Striving together works best, that is, pushes the participants to be their best, when the competitors are relatively evenly matched. If the skill level is too different, the impact of striving together is limited and does not provide the wider community with useful information about who is better. It simply was never a contest (or meaningful tournament). Evenly matched competitors, those who are similar in talent and skill, make for a competitive striving. We may enjoy vanquishing a competitor but if we had a steady diet of "patsies" the game would eventually cease to be enjoyable, and our skills would begin to deteriorate. Real competition is always with someone who pushes us. We are both seeking to perform at a higher level and that goal is aided by a competitor of similar ability and experience.

Coordination

The root of the word coordination is the Latin *ordo* meaning to set in order, to arrange in succession. When "co" is added, the word means to set in order with someone. As with cooperation and competition, the act of arranging things in order or setting priorities can be done alone or with someone. And as with the other "co-actions," the fact of doing something with another person makes more complex both the task and the emotions associated with it. Coordinating with someone, like cooperating with them, involves considering their views or thoughts. Unlike cooperation, which is about aligning interests, coordination is about aligning the order of operations. What comes first, second, and third? Like cooperation, coordination requires both communication and agreement.

It is important to recognize that while each of these words conveys a unique relational activity – working together, striving together, and arranging together – there are shared dimensions as well. Competition clearly involves cooperation. Without a shared commitment to rules, for example, a fair competition is impossible. In the shared interest of pushing each other to run as fast as we can, we must agree on a starting line, a starting and ending point and the acceptable behaviors in between. We may also need to agree on what we are allowed to ingest! Similarly, coordination requires some level of cooperation. If we are arranging things with someone else, we certainly need them to work with us. In a work environment many of us have experienced the frustration of trying to coordinate an event or initiative without the full cooperation of the others who are involved.

Dependency

This leads to a final observation about these three experiences (and the words that attempt to capture them). The acts of working, striving, and arranging with another person evoke a wide range of feelings. None is more central than the feelings that come with the dependency that is built into each of these activities. Linguistically this dependency is represented by the prefix "co" or "com." It is possible, of course, to work alone and to put things in order alone. It is even possible to compete with one's (previous) self. Once we seek to describe an activity that is done with another person, the fact of our reliance on that person for the accomplishment of the task becomes part of the task itself. Alone we do not have to consider another person. Alone I do not have to depend on another's effort or skill level or opinion. But for work that involves someone else, these considerations are part of the work. Our ability to function effectively in a relationship likely determines our success in completing the task.

Collaboration is no exception to this observation. If anything, collaboration represents a more intense mutual dependency than cooperation, competition, and coordination. The roots of the word collaboration are fascinating for what they reveal about the experience of collaboration by the people who, across time, built the language to convey the experience. The "labor" part of the word comes from the Latin *labi* which means to glide or slip or fall. It is curious at first glance that "labor" seems to be based not on work (*opus*) but on slipping. The path from slipping (*labi*) to labor takes us first to *lapsus*, to slip repeatedly, and to risk falling. *Labi* is also recruited (linguistically) to mean labor because of the weight that might cause someone to slip or fall but certainly causes them to tire. The Latin word *laborare* means to bend under a heavy weight. When we say, "They labor under the assumption that life is fair," the word "under" takes us back to the Latin root of labor, the effort needed to stay upright when carrying a heavy weight, the effort needed to keep from stumbling or tiring and crumbling. Labor is hard work, filled with risk and strain.

When we labor with someone, the risk and strain increase. Added to the weight of the task is the risk of depending upon another person to hold up (literally) their half of the burden. When someone asks me to co-teach a course, I feel both the potential for synergy or load sharing and the extra time and energy that will be required to manage the joint teaching. This is reinforced by the reactions from my colleagues. "Co-teaching is much more work than teaching alone." It is not only the burden I worry about but the constant assessment of whether I am doing too much or too little relative to my partner. In all honesty, I worry about whether my reputation as an educator will be affected by my partner's performance. When that partner is a teaching assistant or is junior to me, I worry less than if my teaching partner is a peer or is senior to me. The worry is an expression of the risk I experience in "laboring" with someone else.

Collaboration Defined

The truth is that in my efforts to formulate a working definition of collaboration, I started with my experience. I knew that my experience of collaboration included moments of satisfaction, support, creativity, and learning. I also knew that collaboration could be tiring, stressful, challenging, and frustrating. When I began to investigate the words used to describe different types of co-working, the eureka moment came when I discovered that *labi* yields both *laborare* (to labor) and *lapsis* (to fall). Suddenly it struck me that the language makers (or more accurately, the generations of language developers) had chosen "collaborate" to describe a working relationship that involved both creativity and accomplishment as well as stress and difficulty precisely because the roots of the word conveyed the "both/and" nature of the experience. Collaborate holds out not only the possibility of creative accomplishment but also the possibility of collapse. The burden may be too heavy or the risks for one or both people may be too great. Collapse is linguistically and experientially part of collaboration. Even when modern usage seems to strip away the risk and burden of collaboration, experience (and a word origin dictionary) tells us that struggle and challenge are still alive in any meaningful collaboration.

In the preceding paragraphs I have occasionally included the word "creative" in my description of collaboration. Creativity will be a central feature of this book's exploration of collaboration going forward, a descriptor that distinguishes collaboration from the other forms of co-working. But creativity is not an explicit part of the etymological history of the word. For my purposes, which include exploring the relational and psychological dynamics of collaboration, and from my experience in collaborations, I have come to believe that creativity is essential to any characterization of collaboration. The closest the Latin roots come to creativity is in the description of collaboration as laboring to accomplish something. *Opus* was used, in the medieval period, to describe physical work, the work done by feudal serfs. *Labore* as we have seen was used for a different purpose. Labor was an effort under duress that was aimed at accomplishment. "Labor of love" is a felicitous English phrase that suggests the times when work is more than drudgery or effort. It is an effort that brings forth something new or exciting or special.

It is not a huge leap to imagine why our ancestral language makers, generations of people using words and adapting them to experience, chose the word "labor" (instead of "work") to describe the intensity of the child-birthing process. As one who has only observed, albeit up close, this process, it is clearly painful work, excruciatingly so, filled with stress and risk. It also, thankfully in most cases, accomplishes something both common place and extraordinary, the birth of a child, the final step in a creative process that took months to come to fruition. I have chosen to see creativity in the word labor to more clearly distinguish collaboration from other forms of working together. "Seeing" creativity in collaboration stems from the way collaboration is described by those involved in it: a creative process that sometimes happens when two people work together.

The last piece of the definitional puzzle for collaboration also stems from this description. Does collaboration happen when any two people work together on a stressful, risky task? Is the shared risk and difficult burden of accomplishment enough to spark creativity? Or does the potential for creativity when two people work together depend on more than just effort and opportunity? Here again, the linguistic need for a different word than cooperate (work together) suggests that merely working together is not what is being expressed in the word collaborate. It could be that the "slip and fall" risk contained in the root is the additional meaning. But collaboration also adds accomplishment to the work theme. What fuels that creative accomplishment, I believe, are the differences each person brings to the working relationship.

These differences make creativity possible. Across numerous interviews with collaborators, dozens of written accounts of collaborative relationships and my own experience with professional collaboration, it is the role of difference that stands out as the defining feature of a mutually creative activity. When people say their relationship "just clicked" they most often mean that their different contributions meshed. I have never read about, nor talked to collaborators who credited their similarity with driving the creativity in their relationship. As we shall see, like effort and sharing the load, difference is necessary but not sufficient. Merely putting two people together with one or more dimensions of difference does not guarantee a successful collaboration. But without diverse backgrounds, perspectives, talents, and skills creativity in a relationship is impossible.

I will use the following working definition: collaboration is a creative connection across differences. Each piece of the definition expresses an important and essential element of a collaborative relationship. In the next three chapters, we will explore each of the three elements. First, we will interrogate what is meant by "creativity" so that we have a foundation for identifying a particular relationship as a collaboration. Second, we will look at the types of differences that people bring to their collaborations. These differences are the key to understanding the ebb and flow of most collaborations. They can both stimulate and alienate. They are at the heart of the potential and the challenge inherent in working together to create. Finally, we will examine what kind of interpersonal connection incubates a creative process. What are the characteristics of relationships that lead to creative products?

Endnotes

1 Morton Deutsch and Peter T. Coleman, *The Handbook of Conflict Resolution: Theory and Practice* (San Francisco: Jossey-Bass, 2000), pp. 21–40.
2 John von Neumann and Oskar Morgenstern, *Theory of Games and Economic Behavior* (Princeton: Princeton University Press, 2007).
3 John F. Nash, 'The Bargaining Problem,' *Econometrica* 18, no. 2 (1951): 155–162.
4 Richard Schell, *Bargaining for Advantage: Negotiation Strategies for Reasonable People* (New York: Penguin, 1999).
5 Roy Lewicki, Bruce Barry, and David Saunders, *Negotiation* (Boston: McGraw-Hill, 2006).

Chapter 3

Creativity

Creativity is at the heart of our working definition of collaboration. Creativity that emerges from collective work *is* collaboration. Before we delve into the sources of creativity in relationships (what is added to a cooperative relationship that allows for and makes possible creativity) and the process whereby these ingredients give rise to a creative outcome (what exactly happens in a collaborative relationship), we will look at the central concept itself.

Human curiosity about creativity dates to antiquity. Every social group has an origin story, an account of how they came into existence. In many cases, the origin story includes how other aspects of our world came into existence, physical and metaphysical. Origin stories are also called creation stories. They involve a narrative about how something came from nothing. The second word of the Hebrew Bible, for example, is "created." The origin account which follows is explicit that something, everything, was created from nothing. It is a question that is asked and answered in many cultures: How were we and everything around us created? Chinese origin stories involve the relationship between *yin* and *yang* that gives rise to the vital energy that permeates the world called *qi*. The interaction or balance of *yin* and *yang*, dark and light, cold and hot, female and male, wet and dry creates the universe. Origin stories persist, adjust, and develop as we learn about creative processes in the world, from what creates leprosy to what explains the existence of the natural forces that shape our world.

In the Western world, the question of how something can be created from nothing, specifically how something living can arise from something inanimate, persisted for 2,000 years. Aristotle and his contemporaries were aware of sexual reproduction in humans and animals. Yet the origins of some animals were thought to be spontaneously generated from non-living matter.[1] This "hypothesis" was not disproven until the nineteenth century when the methods and instruments of early modern science were applied to the age-old question of creation.

DOI: 10.4324/9781032701998-3

Questions about the source of human creativity also have ancient roots. The Greeks imagined that the muses were the sources of inspiration for human creativity. Though often associated with the arts, according to the Greeks, the muses inspired creative work in the sciences and mathematics as well. The key question for human creativity was the same as the key question for origin stories: how something new emerges from something pre-existing? The muse provided one answer: a goddess. The goddesses were external sources of inspiration, whispered insights, or guiding presences that lit the creative flame for humans. In an age when most literary and scientific pursuits were only allowed to men, the muses were female. The muses could have been male, but they weren't. The Greeks undoubtedly knew that creation is a product of difference. Procreation, the combination of male and female to produce a unique offspring, may have served as the foundational example of the creative process. As a result, in the minds of the mythmakers of ancient Greece, a male world may have been seen as incapable of creativity without the presence of the female. The muses answered the riddle of the (pro)creative process.

The Chinese too saw creation both in the natural world and the human world as a product of the interaction of difference. One origin story describes how the interaction of *yin* and *yang* brought everything into existence, *both* stability and chaos were created in the relationship between opposite forces.[2] When these forces are in harmony, creative possibilities are endless. When they are not in balance, the potential for destruction (paradoxically, the creation of the chaotic nothing that predated existence) increases.

The Psychology of Creativity

By the middle of the last century, the curiosity about creative people, creative work, and creative processes found its scientific expression in a psychologist, J. P. Guilford.[3] Guilford was interested in human intelligence and became an expert in measurement, especially the identification and measurement of mental abilities. Much of his work focused on measuring the various components he believed comprised intelligence (there were dozens of such components described in his work). One of his major contributions to the study of human creativity was the concept of divergent thinking, the ability to generate multiple solutions to a problem.[4] Guilford further articulated four components of this cognitive operation. Fluency refers to the number of ideas that a person can generate. Flexibility attempts to assess the different "categories" of ideas a person generates. If all my ideas about problems or challenges were variations of the same theme (e.g., 20 vegetable options for lunch), I would be considered highly fluent but not very flexible (what about meats or fruits?). Elaboration describes the extent to which a person can develop, amplify, and work with ideas. The final component, the most conceptually difficult of the four is originality.

Core to most definitions of creativity is this idea of originality. If I have a lot of ideas (fluent) in many different categories (flexible) and I can develop many of them (elaborate), but they are not original, how could this be called a creative mental operation? But what does "original" mean? What is the relationship between "novel," "new," and "innovative?" When we use these last three words to explain "original" we can find ourselves struggling to differentiate among them.

A "new" weight loss drug, for example, may involve a rather small tweak to an existing molecular therapy that allows the company producing the drug to gain a new patent just as the old one is about to expire. On one hand, this would hardly seem to qualify as original. The resulting drug is like the existing one in most meaningful ways. On the other hand, does the new drug represent a novel approach, extending the productive life of the pre-existing (and presumably, original) drug? Similarly, an "innovation" may not involve anything original; it may be the brilliant combination of old ideas or products in a way that solves a problem more effectively than anything else. Repurposing a t-shirt launching compressed air "cannon" to send canisters of drugs across a border wall is a novel *use* of existing resources (drugs and air cannons) to solve a problem.[5] Does the combination of familiar elements qualify as something original? If so, can we substitute "innovative" for "original"? Perhaps, but "innovative" seems to involve problem-solving whereas "original" could apply to a piece of art, a creation that does not involve solving a problem.

To make matters more complicated, the use of the word "original" to describe a piece of art or a work product almost always seems to be an exaggeration. Most originality is founded upon and derives from the accumulated work of what has come before. Almost nothing that humans create is created *de novo*. In some cases, the work springs from the creator's own previous attempts. In other cases, it is rooted in cultural or professional practice. In still other cases, the work of countless others informed the ultimate creation.

The challenges continue as we explore a second dimension of creativity identified by psychological researchers, the requirement that the creative product be "appropriate" to a problem or task in the environment.[6] Put in slightly different words, the product of a creative process must be useful in some way. The rationale for this second dimension is that without anchoring the creative process in utility, the originality dimension of creativity might become absurdly irrelevant to our understanding of the concept. Standing on your head while singing the national anthem at a sporting event may be original but is it creative? (If some of you are thinking "Yes!" and imagining the event as a form of performance art, intended to convey the artist's view of the world, hang on to that thought.) From the perspective of utility and appropriateness, standing on your head can seem unrelated to any problem or task. But if the same activity happened in a museum of modern art (rather than in an arena or stadium) it might seem both original and related to the "task" of social commentary, a task often "worked on" using artistic methods. It could easily be described as creative.

Adding appropriateness to the definition of creativity raises more questions. Is creativity the same as effective problem-solving? Is the phrase "creative problem solving" redundant when solving a problem is a part of what we mean by creative? Or does adding "task" and "problem" point us to the involvement of environment and culture in how we see and define creative products? In the example of the inverted crooner, the context makes all the difference. In the sports arena, most people might think the person singing while standing on his head is strange, zany, crazy, drunk, or inappropriate. In the Museum of Modern Art, most people might reflect on what the artist is trying to say and on her choice of subject. (And when we say, "most people" who exactly are they, and who exactly do we have in mind?)

James Kaufman, in his introduction to the academic work on creativity – *Creativity 101* – proposes the four P's as a way of describing the many facets of creativity on which research is being carried out: product, process, person, and press (environment).[7] What Guilford might once have conceptualized as characteristics of the *person's* mental operations is now contextualized by the characteristics of the creative product, the creative process, and the environment in which both the person and the process exist.

The product is often regarded as the central feature, the novel or original, tangible result of "a person's creative *process* influenced by the *press* (aka environment)." Without a product, there is no real meaning to the concept of creativity. How we assess a product to determine its originality or novelty is a topic of both discussion and research, but some method of assessment would seem to be crucial. There is no product without a person. For many, a single person is the source of the creative product. Something about who they are and how they think is essential to the creative process. And this too is the subject of much study and the domain of many educational activities. Many of us have attended workshops designed to stimulate our creativity and these workshops involve steps in a process aimed at developing what Guilford called our fluency, flexibility, and capacity for elaboration.

Are we to conclude that creativity is a process made up of many distinct "sub" processes, some related to the mind of the individual person and others related to the characteristics of the environment? Do these subprocesses each describe a different aspect of creativity? Or does our struggle to define creativity lead us to pull apart a phenomenon we all know when we see it, pulling it apart in a way that obscures its fundamental character rather than revealing it? Does a precise definition matter to anyone other than those of us inside academe? Can we use many synonymous words to get at the meaning of creativity without losing some fundamental understanding of the process? Does the desire for conceptual and linguistic precision reduce the power of the concept itself or enhance it? If we want to understand the creative process and the elements that contribute to it, do we need to be precise?

Defining Creativity

Plucker, Beghetto, and Dow (2004) proposed a definition of creativity that incorporated the key elements of research in the area. "Creativity is the interaction among aptitude, process, and environment by which an individual or group produces a perceptible product that is both novel and useful as defined within a social context."[8] Their definition includes individual as well as contextual factors, novelty, and utility as underlying criteria while simultaneously acknowledging that an "interaction" of all these forces, a "secret sauce" yet unidentified, plays a critical role.

One question at the heart of this definition of creativity is: "Who decides?" Who determines which aptitudes determine creative thinking? Who creates the models of creative processes and evaluates them? Who determines experts for use in expert assessments of originality or novelty? Who assigns a "usefulness" or "appropriate" score to a creative product? It is tempting to answer these questions empirically, by looking at convergences among people. Most creative people have the characteristic "X" so perhaps this characteristic is an important element. Most people agree that "Y" is a crucial ingredient in novelty. Most people find product "Z" to be more useful than its predecessors. But this brings us back to the nagging question of who we mean by "most people." Who are we asking and in what social and cultural context?

The last line in the Plucker, Beghetto, and Dow definition tells us that creativity is contextually defined. It points to what we might have suspected when we began this brief review of the meaning of creativity. The essential elements of creativity (e.g., originality and utility) are heavily determined by the human environment that is making the constituent judgments. History provides us with the most obvious examples of this reality. Copernicus's theory that the Sun was at the center of the solar system was original and useful in 1543 but by 1969 it was neither. A clever (original and entertaining) joke in one context can fall flat or offend in another, experienced as neither novel nor entertaining. Were we to survey the human environment concerning either of these events, our understanding of creativity would reflect the social context as much as it would be influenced or defined by it. Rather than seeking an "objective" or "universal" definition of creativity, we could use the Plucker, Beghetto, and Dow versions to embrace the subjective or human consensual aspect of the concept.

Shift in Focus: Creativity as a Relational Concept

The aim of this book is to deepen our understanding of the dynamics of two-person collaborations. For our purposes, I will attempt to shift our understanding of creativity from an activity that happens primarily within an individual to one that is relational at its core. Human beings are social animals, raised, educated, and socialized throughout life by the various others around them. A child's drawing builds on what she has been exposed to, what she has seen, and how she has learned to make sense of what surrounds her. There is no doubt that her unique combination of neurons and coordinated muscle tissue contribute to her art, but even these neurons are the result of contributions of genetic material from others! The praise (or criticism) of her "original" art shapes what she is likely to produce in the future.

As we grow, what we "produce" is further shaped by other relationships. Parents, teachers, classmates, friends, and colleagues are sources of stimulation and feedback, whether solicited or not. The cultural norms that form the backdrop of our interpersonal relations also contribute to the way our minds process information, articulate aspirations, and envision future possibilities. Whether we find ourselves in agreement with these cultural mores or at war with them, their existence exerts a force on us. For human beings, there is no other possibility. We grow up in and among others.

Almost anything we produce can be seen as something built on the efforts of others. A woodworker creates a unique cutting board with the skill and knowledge handed down through an apprenticeship relationship. It might also have been inspired by a cutting board created by someone else. In some cases, the woodworker may have swapped ideas with a fellow woodworker such that the final product is an amalgam of their contributions. Even in the world of innovation and discovery, the person associated with an invention rarely worked alone and even more rarely was unaware of the work being done by others around them. Jonas Salk will forever be associated with the discovery of the polio vaccine, but the work of many scientific labs preceded Salk's efforts, and many labs were working on this problem at the same time, even sharing (through journals, conferences, and conversations) their observations and hypotheses. Had Salk not "discovered" the vaccine someone else would have because this creativity was supported both by the others in his lab and the others in his scientific environment.[9]

Humans are created through a procreative rather than a replicative process. Two unique individuals contribute some, but not all, of their uniqueness to put in motion the development of a third unique individual. This is the essence of the collaborative process, and it continues throughout human life. One need only imagine a human being raised in total isolation to stare into the absurdity of any creation happening outside a relationship. First, a human being could not survive in isolation. Unlike turtles, who lay their eggs in the sand and swim back out to sea, leaving the hatchlings to fend for themselves, human offspring are raised by others until they are capable, physically and mentally, of survival. Second, their ability to survive is less about instinct (as it is with turtles) and more about learned behaviors. Those who do not learn do not survive. It is upon the foundation of these learnings that "new" inventions, aids to survival, are created. Perhaps there are true "AHA!" moments, ideas that spring from whole cloth, but they are rare if they exist at all. Many apples had fallen from many trees in front of Newton's eyes for many years. We tell the story about his *individual* discovery as if it were a moment of insight. More likely, Newton had been observing the natural world with curiosity for decades, curiosity nurtured by others and informed by the fruits (or failures) of *their* curiosity. The story of Newton's discovery renders invisible the role of relationships with others in his creativity.

A relational view of creativity will also depart from the efforts to measure and assess creativity objectively (or as a consensus among expert observers) by locating the definition of creativity in the relationship rather than outside it. As we have noticed, one of the challenges in assessing creativity is delineating its many components both within and surrounding the creative individual. At one point Kaufman reports that Guilford had identified 120 separate mental abilities comprising creativity.[10] Measuring these factors, differentiating them from each other, determining the importance of each for our understanding of the concept of creativity, and then *recombining* them to construct a valid and reliable indication of creativity must have been daunting.

The validation process alone has proved challenging since it often hinges on assembling "experts" to assess the novelty or originality of creative products. Experts are people who have demonstrated command of a particular field or area of knowledge. On the one hand, this would seem to position them to recognize novelty in the field because they know what the field contains. On the other hand, their knowledge is historical by necessity, and while giving them the background to assess originality, the same knowledge might "frame" their assessment of new products coming into the field. Physicians, for example, are susceptible to missing diagnoses because reading a patient's chart can cause them to frame a symptom to "fit in" with a pre-existing condition.[11,12]

More broadly, experts are embedded in the period in which they live. This cultural environment influences not only the creative product itself but the assessment of the creative product as well. Imagine Samuel Beckett (a Nobel Prize winner in literature in the twentieth century) producing *Waiting for Godot* in Elizabethan times. It is unlikely that this pioneering work would have been appreciated when viewed alongside Shakespeare and his contemporaries. Experts (theater critics) at the time might not have deemed the play original or profound but rather silly and incomprehensible. Many of Shakespeare's plays, in contrast, though written in the late sixteenth and early seventeenth centuries, are still regarded by contemporary experts (theater critics) as masterpieces of drama. Does this mean that Shakespeare's work was creative and Beckett's not? No, it rather points to the reality that judging creativity, even for "experts," is deeply embedded in a cultural context. As a result, an objective assessment of the essence of creativity may be impossible.

A Different Conceptualization

How would a "relational" view of creativity define the concept? Such a view of creativity locates its source in the relationship between two or more people rather than in the mind of a single individual. It also views with skepticism any attempt to objectively assess core elements of a creative process (e.g., originality and novelty). Instead, our working definition of creativity for purposes of exploring two-person collaboration is deceptively simple: *creativity, as determined by the two people involved, is a process that results in a product neither individual could have developed alone*. Before we explore the implications of this definition there is one caveat. The "product" in this definition cannot be merely the result of effort or some other additive capacity. For example, two of us can produce a larger pile of sand on the beach in five minutes than either of us could have alone. We will not consider this large pile of sand a creative product, for although it was something produced by the pair that neither could have produced alone, it is simply a function of effort or capacity. If we build a sandcastle that neither of us, *by our own assessment*, would have envisioned or constructed alone, this will fit our definition. Or, had we, together, developed an original, *to us*, method of gathering and piling sand on the beach, this method could be considered a creative product if we both agreed that neither of us would have developed it alone.

We can now examine Kaufman's four P's (person, product, process, and press/environment) through the lens of a relational conception of creativity. The *person* becomes a *relationship* and our focus shifts from the intellectual and cognitive abilities of an individual to the characteristics of this relationship. With this shift come questions about these relationships.

Do the people involved have similar or different personal or professional backgrounds (in relation to each other)? Do they have different strengths and weaknesses (in relation to each other)? Are the two people in the same physical space often or infrequently (not a question one would ask about an individual)? We can then ask how these, and many other descriptors of the *relationship*, contribute to the product that emerges from it.

Our relational definition of creativity helps address the challenging aspects of determining a creative *product.* The work that two people undertake together is deemed useful and, if necessary, novel or original by the people themselves. If there is a problem to be solved (creatively), the decision to undertake the task is made together. If the problem requires an original or novel approach, the people involved make this determination and then work together to produce it. It is the relationship (rather than the individual or an expert) that has the final say about the originality of the product. This may seem absurd at first glance. Isn't the proof of novelty or originality to be found in the environment, in the people who taste the cake, or use the mousetrap, or purchase the sculpture? But as we have discussed, this "consensus" view of creativity is not only fraught with cultural and historical ambiguity, but it also may miss the point when applied to a two-person collaboration. If two people produce a new mousetrap, a mousetrap that works, a mousetrap that neither could have produced in isolation, does it matter if no one buys it?

Most of us have had the experience of working on something with another person and creating something that we did not envision or imagine when we began the work. It emerged from the give and take of conversation, the heat and light of conflicting views, the ways in which the ideas and skills of one person stimulated the thinking of the other. And most of us know what that felt like. We may have walked away amazed at what we created together, amazed that we produced something that each of us alone could not have conceived. If it turned out that two people down the hallway had, coincidentally, produced the same idea, the same product, the same mousetrap, would this make our work any less creative? It might be labeled as less creative by someone looking at what came out of the two rooms since the products were identical. But from the perspective of the two people involved, a perspective that seeks to understand how *relationships* produce original work, the creative act was real, a reality that is not changed by what others produce.

Procreation, the creation of a child from two parents, does not depend on what that child is, what it becomes, or even if it is genetically identical to its twin. As a foundational metaphor for two-person creativity, procreation emphasizes that the creative "product" is defined by the fact that neither of the people involved could have done it alone. In humans, procreation most often results in a single genetically unique outcome, but the uniqueness of the child is not the defining emotional or intellectual aspect of the "product." The fact that millions of children are born every day, that they are, especially at birth, much more similar than different, and that their "utility" is yet to manifest itself, does not diminish the creativity represented by each one.

Within a relational framework, the *process* aspect of creativity also becomes a matter of relationship dynamics rather than a question of mental facility or information processing. In their work together, do the two people listen to each other? Do they fight, struggle, or disagree? If so, when, and why? How do they manage various forms of conflict? Do they care about each other? Are they friends? If not, does this matter? Are there recurring emotional or relational patterns in their work together such as envy, competition, and mutual validation? If so, how do these patterns contribute to or detract from what they produce together? Even more broadly, how do the two people manage co-creating? How do they handle decision-making, time investment, task allocation, and logistics? When an individual is sitting alone working on a project, none of these questions arise.

Finally, our understanding of the *press* or *environment* in which the work occurs also changes as we shift focus to the creative relationship. Practically and concretely, the primary environmental factor is the collaborator. Unlike the societal factors that may influence the creative process, the needs, trends, technologies, and problems that surround an individual, the most immediate and intimate manifestation of these factors is the other. There are two major ways in which the other brings the environment into a creative relationship. First, the other brings with them a micro-environment, a personal version of the larger societal factors. Their opinions, knowledge, and experience will be affected by what exists in society, but their unique take on this wider culture becomes part of their interpersonal relationship with a co-creator. Conversations between collaborators are thus also conversations between their respective micro-environments. Each interpersonal interaction is simultaneously an interaction between these micro-environments. The interpersonal relationship makes the influence of the environment intimate and concrete. The environment shows up not as an abstract characterization or a media-moderated symbol but as a personal preference or conviction, a strong revulsion or attraction, or a critical or appreciative stance on one or more issues of the day. All of these become a very real part of the creative process between two people.

The second concrete way that the environment is brought into the creative relationship is through the groups to which each collaborator belongs. These groups represent the niche or niches in the broader society that each collaborator inhabits. As much as the individual personalities of the collaborators, these groups funnel the environment directly into the relationship. In the United States, a Black person and a White person working together bring with them the historical and current relationship between Blacks and Whites. In a manufacturing organization, an engineer and a salesperson collaborating on a project bring with them the historical and current relationships between their departments. A singer and a songwriter, a cell biologist and a geneticist, and a male and female entrepreneur all bring groups with them, many not just one, and each of these groups has a history with other groups. The attitudes formed by groups about and toward other groups are imported into the creative relationship.

As we will explore later in this book, the intimate presence of the environment is both a boon and a potential threat to the creative relationship. The potential for synergy as well as the possibility of conflict and discord are both present. In most creative relationships, the groups to which the collaborators belong are the source of the pair's creativity. All groups educate and train their members on how to see and relate to the world. All groups see the world differently (sometimes radically so and sometimes only moderately so) which translates into different educational foundations for their members. Afro-Caribbean music does not exist without African music and Caribbean music and, like all other creative blends, the process by which these different group influences are put together is a creative one, the result is something neither group (nor group representative) could have produced alone.

Finally, this relational view of creativity directs us to attend primarily two aspects of the collaborative relationship if we want to understand the creative process: (1) the nature of the differences that are represented in the two people involved and (2) the nature of the relationship between them that enables these differences to contribute to their mutual work. The next two chapters examine these two aspects.

Endnotes

1 'Spontaneous Generation in Antiquity – TAPA 51:101–115 (1920),' penelope.uchicago.edu. Retrieved May 22, 2023.
2 Stephan Feuchtwang, *Religions in the Modern World: Traditions and Transformations* (New York: Routledge, 2016), p. 150, ISBN 978-0-415-85881-6.
3 Joy Paul Guilford, 'Creativity,' *American Psychologist* 5, no. 9 (1950): 444–454.
4 Joy Paul Guilford, *The Nature of Human Intelligence* (New York: McGraw-Hill, 1967).
5 Christian Terweisch and Karl Ulrich, *Innovation Tournaments: Creating and Selecting Exceptional Opportunities* (Boston: Harvard Business Press, 2009).
6 Robert J. Sternberg, *Handbook of Creativity* (Cambridge: Cambridge University Press, 1999).

7 James Kaufman, *Creativity 101* (New York: Springer, 2009).
8 Jonathan Plucker, Ronald Beghetto, and Gail Dow, 'Why Isn't Creativity More Important to Educational Psychologists?,' *Educational Psychologist* 39, no. 2 (2004): 83–96.
9 John Rowan Wilson, *Margin of Safety* (New York: Doubleday, 1963).
10 James Kaufman, *Creativity 101* (New York: Springer, 2009).
11 Jingjing Gong, 'A Review of Framing in Medical Decision Making,' *Journal of Health Psychology* 18, no. 4 (2013): 530–538.
12 Jennifer Blumenthal-Barby and Heather Krieger, 'Cognitive Biases and Heuristics in Medical Decision Making: A Critical Review Using a Systematic Review Strategy,' *Medical Decision Making* 35, no. 4 (2015): 539–557.

Chapter 4

Difference

The creativity in a two-person collaboration is fueled by the differences between them. In most cases, a commonality brings them together, sometimes a shared objective or aspiration, other times simply a shared appreciation of working with each other. But their differences provide a collaborative relationship with the raw material for what they create. In artistic collaborations, these differences are rooted in the component parts of the artistic creation. Opera, for example, requires a librettist and a composer because opera is the marriage of poetry and music. In rare cases, the same person can produce both the libretto and the score, but this is unusual since the preparation for each of these contributions is significant. Hugo Von Hofmannsthal was a serious playwright and poet when he met Richard Strauss by then an accomplished composer. The practice at the time (early twentieth century), and one that had existed for decades, was that the creation of an opera was the work of two domains of expertise. This practice has continued. The Rogers and Hammerstein collaboration in the American musical theater is legendary.

In the work world too, collaborations are often most successful when two people bring different skills to the enterprise, skills which, taken together, are necessary for the success of the undertaking. Many entrepreneurial ventures, when they are founded by two people, involve partners who come from different, equally important, domains. A technical person and a salesperson or a financial person and an operations person. Sean and Emily (I have changed their names) were both young business school graduates when they founded a company together. What drew them to each other was not primarily their shared drive and impatience, but rather their differences. She was technically and financially inclined. He liked playing with ideas and generating proposals for them to think about. "Emily is the confident, technically skilled one of us, but also an unconventional thinker. I tend to be the one who likes to play with ideas."[1]

The role of difference in the creative process makes intuitive sense. An individual, even one engaged in a creative effort, is constrained by their

DOI: 10.4324/9781032701998-4

unique characteristics. The challenge for individual artists is not to become "stale" since the risk of merely replicating one's work is always present. Individuals seek stimulation from other sources (other people, other disciplines, other aspects of life) because the essence of procreation is the combination of differences. Cloning or replicating is not a creative activity as we have defined it. Cellular replication, for example, requires only one cell, and it produces a copy of that one cell (marred only by mutations or transcription errors). Procreation is precisely not replication nor simple reproduction. Two different entities giving birth to something that neither could have produced alone is a powerful metaphor for human collaboration more broadly.

Temperament and Style

What kind of differences are we talking about when we examine human collaboration? The first difference noticed is often a difference in style or temperament. One person is organized and detail oriented. The other is laid back to the point of absent-mindedness. One person is sociable, voluble, and engaging. The other is a loner or perhaps a bit of a misanthrope. One person works best at night. The other is a morning person. All these observed differences are variations on the "odd couple" motif, opposites who not only coexist but find some mutual benefit in their vastly different ways of being in the world. Tony is the head coach of a women's athletic team. Jenny has coached with Tony for decades. (Here again, I have changed the names.) It is a collaboration in all the ways we have described. "Anyone in the field knows that I could not have done this without Jenny. Anyone who knows," says Tony. "I'm the ideas person, Jenny is the execution. She is organized (and I am not). I knew exactly what I needed. She was independent, driven and didn't need a lot of guidance and I wasn't good at what she was good at." Jenny describes Tony as "nice, the schmoozer type, softer and more political whereas I tend to be more forceful, stronger and demanding, willing to confront what needs to be confronted."[2]

Or take the example of the spontaneous slob who contributes the occasional exciting detour from the straight and narrow. Continuous spontaneity runs the risk of remaining unfocused, never allowing the collaboration to follow through on the myriad steps that bring anything to fruition. But too much obsession with workflow and "deliverables" runs the risk of prematurely stifling potentially stimulating ideas or approaches. Differences in temperament, in and of themselves, do not always contribute to a collaboration. They may simply be an irritant or an enjoyable stimulant in a relationship. As with other dimensions of difference discussed below, the key element of these style or temperament differences is that the difference contributes to the creative work.

Talent and Skill

Perhaps more obvious in its contribution to a collaboration is a difference in talent or skill. When a librettist and a composer come together to create an opera, the work benefits from their respective expertise. Iconic opera owes its status to the unique combination of lyricism and musical expression. In the work world, the relationship between a design engineer and a manufacturing expert can create a product that is both appealing and profitable. These differences in skill often have the clearest connection to collaborative work. Most poets cannot compose music. Many athletic coaches were not great players. Different skill sets, by their very essence, make collaboration possible.

Bundini Brown was, off and on over many years, Mohammed Ali's corner man. Ali was the premier heavyweight fighter of his era. He boxed with intelligence, skill, and flare. Often lighter than his opponent, the speed of his hands and feet brought him numerous world titles. He had an entire entourage that attended him at his training camp, arranged his fights, cooked his meals, sparred with him, ran with him, and traveled with him. Bundini Brown's skill was his ability to motivate. He could not box, but he could inspire. He did this in numerous, mostly verbal, ways. At times exhorting Ali. At other times reminding Ali that he had a destiny. Bundini's inventiveness with language bonded the two men. Not only could Bundini motivate Ali inside the ring, but he also inspired Ali's poetic gifts. Together they crafted the rhetorical flourishes that came to symbolize Ali. The rhyming schemes that predicted the round in which Ali would knock out his opponent as well as the couplet (originally a quatrain) that became Ali's moniker ("Float like a butterfly, sting like a bee") were created with Brown.[3]

Brown's contribution to Ali's success was founded on his understanding of how Ali's mind worked. Where others saw strength, bravado, and power, Brown discerned the Champ's fears and anxieties. Brown's encouragement of Ali, rooted in a spiritual view of the world that fed Ali the confidence he craved and needed, was exactly what Ali needed. Paired with Ali's boxing acumen and courage, Bundini's talents brought Ali success in the ring.

Less precise but often present in a collaboration are qualities of the mind, or how the two individuals think. Smith and I are a good example of two people whose minds work differently. The first time I heard words like cybernetics, metonymy, liminal, and morpho stasis come out of a serious adult's mouth was when Smith introduced me to them. There is a bit of the preacher in him, and his mind is as curious about metaphysics as it is about physics. He is as comfortable with mystery and the realm of the unknown as he is with mastery and mathematics. If Smith has some preacher in him, I am the rabbi in our relationship. I tend toward exegesis, dissecting what's in front of me. If I cannot see it, touch it, or feel it, I'm skeptical about whether it exists. But the two different qualities of our minds, when mixed energetically, were wonderfully stimulating if not always comfortable. The distinction between morpho stasis and morpho genesis (when I finally understood it) made my mind conceptualize theories of individual and organizational change in ways that I had not imagined before.

In a similar vein, intuitive and analytic are words used to capture the different ways a person approaches a problem or analyzes a decision. Intuitive approaches are holistic, taking into account a number of aspects of the situation without necessarily examining each one in detail. Intuition is not a supernatural gift, but rather the result of accumulated experience and knowledge. Analytic approaches, as the term implies, tend to break the problem or decision into its component parts, evaluating each one in turn, to arrive at a solution or course of action. Each approach comes with risks and benefits.

The risks of the intuitive approach involve "missing" something important because of the lack of systematic attention to parts of the task. The collaboration might miss unconscious biases (e.g., the tendency to ignore information that disconfirms a belief, the tendency to exaggerate risky outcomes in favor of secure options). A commitment to scrupulous examination of the collaboration's assumptions and choices is the only possible protection against such biases. A collaboration might also miss creative opportunities that can only be found through rigorous examination and re-examination of familiar and seemingly inconsequential findings. In the world of scientific discovery those who disregard the "negative" findings of a "failed" experiment and move too quickly to the next one, can find themselves missing critical observations that would inform the design and ultimate success of subsequent experiments.

The risks of the analytic approach lie in the distortion that happens when we take an idea or proposal or concept and break it down, reduce it, to its component parts. If one collaborator has an idea for something that does not already exist (a dimension of creativity) and their collaborative partner breaks the idea down into parts that, when reassembled, "prove" that the idea cannot work, the chances of creating something new can disappear. It is entirely possible that a new idea is not feasible. Most new ideas, in fact, are not. But the process of analysis is itself based on concepts and methods (physical or intellectual) that are rooted in our current understanding of any situation (our understanding of the art, science, logic, and probability). Creativity often means questioning these understandings not always simply employing them. Rigorous analysis has its place in any creative process, but it can limit that creative process as well. It is clear as we describe these two mental approaches that the combination has the potential to avoid the risks and maximize the benefits of both.

Complementarity

This brings us to complementarity. Much is made of the individual characteristics described above. Differences in temperament, skill, talent, and mental approach are almost always a part of the way collaborative relationships are characterized. Perhaps this is because such differences are always present. Perhaps it is because when we see a collaboration we look for the ways in which the individuals involved complement each other. We intuitively know, from our own experience being in collaborations and watching others, that complementarity is key to understanding the creative work of these relationships. The differences we notice are not random. They augment each other, filling in gaps, such that the two working together are capable of much more than each of them alone. "These two men *[Gilbert and Sullivan]* who had thus been brought together were radically dissimilar in upbringing, outlook, and temperament: their characters were antipathetic and complementary." [4] If this were not the case, we might not notice either the relationship or its product. It is not that these individual differences are not present in other relationships, maybe in most, but rather that in collaborative relationships the complementarity of the difference is an advantage in the creative process. We see the creative product and we look again and notice this complementarity.

When my limitations are offset by your possibilities the combination (if handled well) can create an outcome neither of us is capable of alone. When my background or training is different from yours and both are relevant to the task at hand, the possibilities expand beyond what each of us might be able to imagine alone. When the questions I ask about the problem to be solved are different from the questions you ask, the potential for a discovery that might have eluded either of us becomes real. Complementary differences create relationships that can exceed the creativity of the individuals involved.

"Home Groups"

Individual-level differences alone, while stimulating (and by turns frustrating), are not the only source of complementary difference in most collaborative relationships. They are often not the most powerful or important. As we have discussed, human beings are raised, socialized, and educated by groups. Initially, groups support each of us with food and protection but quickly this support takes the form of "instructions" that aid us in our growth and survival. Some of this is quite basic and begins in the family or community into which we are born. We learn what plants to avoid, what interesting holes in the wall not to touch, when to poke a pet, and when to back away or hold out an upturned palm. Other aspects of what we are taught are more subtle. How do we address older people and what is appropriate to say or wear in different settings? What is ethical behavior and when, if ever, are unethical actions justified? Some of these instructions are explicit, while others are internalized from our experience and observation. Because we are raised by different families and different communities, what we learn from years of instruction will be different.

As we grow, these "home groups,"[5] the ones instructing us, multiply. Some of us go to a Montessori pre-school and others to a church daycare. Then, elementary school and youth groups, sports teams, and chess clubs. We spend our time with formal and informal groups, and all of them offer us some instruction about the world, how to view it, and how to navigate our way through it. Like any instruction, we may choose to make the lessons our own or reject them, but the groups to which we belong are a powerful influence on who we are and, importantly, what we bring to our relationships. Our schooling, the work we find, and, if lucky, the work we choose, further shape us. In an essential way, we represent the various groups that have taught us when we interact with others. This representation is unique to each of us. Two of us may learn different things from the same group experience (third grade, summer camp, military training, graduate school). And we all have a unique combination of group experiences. When we collaborate with another person, the parts of who we are that are most present in those collaborations are the influences of the groups that shaped us.

We can classify the types of groups that influence what we bring to creative relationships into three broad categories: functional, hierarchical, and identity.[6] The first two groups are often used in describing modern, bureaucratic organizations. Functional groups are those that share a task or set of tasks. The Accounting Department, the IT department, and the Legal Department are all groups defined by what they do. Specialization in organizations is the driving force behind functional groups, replacing the "generalist" with the benefits of deep and focused specialization. Membership in these groups often requires specific training and one's expertise grows with experience in the function. These groups often meet both inside an organization for the purposes of completing an assignment and across organizations for purposes of education and sharing best practices (e.g., professional associations).

Each of us brings our own talents or predispositions to our functional groups. We may have been born with these talents or taught them or been around others who supported our development in these areas. When this talent is applied to a practical purpose, either within a formal organization (e.g., corporation, small business, non-profit service provider) or as part of a group of people who have come together for a common non-work purpose (e.g., community theater, bird watching society), this functional group becomes part of who we are. The more important the group is to us, the more we are likely to learn the knowledge its members have whether that is about accounting practices in a private sector business or bird migration patterns in the Northeastern United States. The more time we spend with this group, the more we learn and the less time available to us to engage in other groups and to learn from them. Our lives are a series of choices about what we do and who we do it with. These choices connect us to certain groups, deepen the influence of these groups on our lives, and concurrently close off our contact with other groups. In very concrete and obvious ways, we come to know more about our own group (interests, norms, history, and activities) than about the other groups to which we do not belong.

Hierarchical groups in organizations are defined by a shared position in the hierarchy of authority. The care with which organizations strive to place people in titled roles (e.g., Director, Manager, Associate Director, Assistant Vice President) testifies to the perceived importance of these roles and often translates into responsibilities, training opportunities, and of course, compensation. In some cases, members of this group meet and work together (e.g., a senior management team or a first-line supervisor training session) but often hierarchical groups are meaningful to their members because they share a position in an organizational structure and, as a result, share a set of pressures, tasks, and challenges.

Like functional groups, hierarchical groups can be based in an organization or more broadly derived from the power relations in a culture or society. Hierarchy in organizations is usually easy to identify. Titles and rank let everyone know who is in which group and how to relate to people in different hierarchical groups. In addition, the titles also convey that one is "promoted" into these groups by those members of the group who occupy roles further up the hierarchy (e.g., job promotions, academic promotions, military promotions). Cultural hierarchies can have just as strong an influence on how we see the world (and how the world sees us) but "local" cultural knowledge is often required to recognize these groups. A name or a school affiliation, for example, can signal one's place in a cultural hierarchy. The legacy of cultural history is often a hierarchical arrangement of groups and, by implication, the individuals within them.

Like functional groups, the time we spend in a particular hierarchical group expands our understanding of that group's experience while limiting our understanding of other groups at different hierarchical locations in the organization or the culture. A popular television series called *Undercover Boss* illustrates the fact that people at the top of most organizational hierarchies have little understanding of what work life is like for those at the bottom. The same could be said about the people at the bottom of the organization. Neither person is at fault for this reality, each is what Smith called "structurally encased"[7] in the reality of their place in the hierarchy. The shared experience of hierarchical roles, whether at the top, bottom, or middle of the hierarchy, shapes what we see and how we interpret the events in our lives. As a result, it also shapes what we bring to a collaboration.

Identity group memberships are those we are born into (and choose to remain in) as well as those groups we choose to join that are not functional or hierarchical. These are group memberships we carry with us from one organizational or social setting to another. They are also more difficult than functional or hierarchical groups to change. Growing up in Pennsylvania, for example, would place me in the group "Pennsylvanians." I will have a particular sense or feeling about this identity, but it is attached to me (and I am attached to it) by virtue of history and experience. I can change this identity by spending most of my adult life in New Jersey or by de-emphasizing my Pennsylvania roots in my daily life, but this change is more difficult than changing jobs, switching hobbies, or deciding to give up my supervisory role to return to the bargaining unit. Our ethnic and racial identities, our gender identity, and our religious upbringing all have an impact on who we are and what we contribute to our relationships (work and non-work). Whether we change our connection to these identity groups or move away from them, whether easy or difficult, what we learn from navigating our memberships in these groups has a lasting influence on us. Lapsed Catholics or secular Jews are describing themselves as both carriers of certain group experiences as well as individuals who have chosen to attenuate (though not totally reject) their connection to these groups.

The portability of identity group memberships, the fact that we bring them with us wherever we go, means that the context can determine the salience of these parts of ourselves. Americans in Paris, for example, find themselves more aware of their American-ness than they are when sitting in a café in New York City. A White person who lives in a predominantly White suburban community who finds himself in a Black neighborhood is likely to become much more aware of his racial identity because of this change in context. Black people living in predominantly White societies and institutions are, similarly, likely to be aware of their racial identity and its implications for their daily lives. Although the fact that context heightens group membership awareness is true for all group memberships, our functional and hierarchical identities are more easily "left behind" than our identity group memberships. When we take off the uniform or sign out for the weekend, we can choose to leave certain memberships in the background of our lives, and in most cases, the world around us will too. But identity group memberships are not attached to organizations, they are alive in our minds (and often in the minds of those around us), and as our minds take in the context, we can feel these aspects of our identity acutely.

These three group-based dimensions of difference overlap. For example, the president of a corporation has come up through a functional part of the organization. As president, they carry this functional history with them, a reality that is not lost on others in that same function when they look up the hierarchy and feel that someone "up there" understands them. This intersection of function and hierarchy has implications both for those who share these group memberships and those who do not. This same president also has several identity group memberships (e.g., age, gender, race, ethnicity). These too influence both the president's perception of the corporate world around them as well as how others in that world view them. The combination of group memberships together with the relationship the president has with each of them creates an almost unique "constellation of differences" that they bring to their work. One's membership in any of these groups can have a significant influence on one's membership in the others. Police officers at the turn of the last century in New York were overwhelmingly Irish. Telephone operators (when they existed) were overwhelmingly female. CEOs of major private sector corporations are overwhelmingly male. In medicine, your specialty (cardiology, pediatrics, primary care, surgery) places you in a hierarchical relationship with other specialties. The combinations of group memberships that are present in each of us mean that any relationship we form is an intersection of hierarchy, function, and identity.

This detour into group-based differences is intended to highlight the contribution to collaboration made by these group memberships, a contribution above and beyond the contributions made by individual-level differences. Groups teach us about the world, about other groups, and about how to understand and interpret history. Group memberships shape what we hear, see, and read. (If we grew up in Pennsylvania, we are more likely to read a newspaper from Pennsylvania, watch leaves turn colors in the Fall, root for Penn State football, and have some family connection to mining and steel.) Group memberships are also likely to influence when and how we talk, and to whom. Engineers are more likely to spend time with engineers than with marketing people. Ex-pats of all kinds seem to find each other in their new national environments. Their conversations often include more reflections on what is happening in their country of origin than might be found in conversations among the native-born. This is no accident. Groups convey culture whether about a function, a hierarchy, or a community.

We bring this cultural "training" and experience, unique within each of us, to any collaboration. The potential for creative work increases with the complementarity of both our individual-level differences and our group-based differences. In a hypothetical extreme, the collaboration of two identical individuals is limited in its creative potential to the individual creativity that each, identically, possesses. Differences in skill, talent, background, training, education, and personal and collective historical awareness have the potential to increase creative output because they open the relationship to exploring a wide array of "combinations," ways of seeing the task that is informed by multiple perspectives. In my family, for example, we enjoy doing crossword puzzles. We have different capacities as individuals and depending upon the theme of the puzzle one or the other of us may have an advantage because our mind sees around the corner of the clues. In addition, my daughters are of a different generation. They read different books and listen to different music. When we work together, the ideas from one person "open doors" for the thinking of the other. I imagine possible answers only after a daughter offers me her take on the clue, a take I would not have considered. Even when both of us could have completed the puzzle alone, the collaboration goes faster and involves many moments when one or the other of us is awed by the door opened by our collaborator.

Complementary differences, at both the individual and group levels, are necessary but not sufficient. If the differences are great, when for example we speak different languages because we come from different cultures (national, ethnic, professional, organizational) we may not be able to make a connection no matter what creative sparks could have been ignited by our differences. If the differences are not only complementary but also conflicting, with the potential for not just sparks but conflagration, we may not be able to get close enough to the differences to establish a creative connection. The challenges to both establishing and maintaining a connection are significant. Our differences can enable creative collaboration, but they can also imperil it. The relationship, the qualities of the connection, is what brings the two individuals together and sustains their work. This is the most relational feature of a collaboration and the subject of the next chapter.

Endnotes

1 Personal interview.
2 Personal interview.
3 Todd Snyder, *Bundini: Don't Believe the Hype* (New York: Hamilcar Publications, 2020).
4 Hesketh Pearson, *Gilbert and Sullivan: A Biography* (New York: Harper & Row, 1935).
5 Leslie A. Curry and David Berg (last author), 'The Role of Group Dynamics in Mixed Methods Health Sciences Research Teams,' *Journal of Mixed Methods Research* 6, no. 1 (2012): 5–20.
6 Clayton P. Alderfer, Group and Intergroup Relations, in J. Richard Hackman and J. Lloyd Suttle (Eds.), *Improving Life at Work* (Santa Monica: Goodyear, 1977), pp. 227–296.
7 Kenwyn K. Smith, *Groups in Conflict: Prisons in Disguise* (Dubuque, Iowa: Kendall/Hunt Publilshing Co., 1982).

Chapter 5

Connection

The collaborative connection, the source of the creativity that comes from the relationship between two people, is born of the differences between them. Most relationships are formed and sustained through shared interests, characteristics, and perspectives. Commonalities create a bond, a set of mutual affinities and the experiences that come with them. They also make the initial stages of any relationship flow easily. Talking about our shared love of running or climbing or cats or food connects us. Most of us enjoy finding and exploring these shared interests. Even the nuanced differences, embedded in a similar passion, connect us because we understand the other through the lens of something we both experience. If, for example, we have a common appreciation of large dogs, your preference for Bernese Mountain Dogs alongside mine for Newfoundlands, often emphasizes our shared interest.

The collaborative connection, in contrast, is founded on the *differences* that each of the two individuals brings to the relationship. As we have already discussed, these differences are the necessary ingredients for the collaborative work. The way the relationship between the collaborators unfolds is the process by which the differences are combined. A relationship with differences at its core requires more effort. Initial conversation can stall or feel awkward, and later discussions are likely to uncover important areas of disagreement or non-overlapping experience. For example, two entering college first-year students might make conversation about how they spent their summer. One relates their recent vacation in the Swiss Alps, but the other might be at a loss for how to continue the conversation because they spent their summer working and can't afford such vacations.

Were these differences in experience and economic circumstance necessary for a collaboration, these two people would have to develop a relationship in which difference rather than similarity connected them. It is not sufficient to merely place different people next to each other or even to assign them a common task. The common phrase in English, "Those two are like oil and water" is often used to indicate that two people (1) are very

DOI: 10.4324/9781032701998-5

different, (2) do not get along, and (3) are likely to separate if left alone for more than a few minutes. Such is the nature of collaboration. Difference provides the raw material and the stimulus for collaborative work, but it can also generate tension and conflict. If these tensions are not handled well, separation and dissolution of the connection are likely. "Opposites attract," but unless they can create a mutually supportive relationship, that initial attraction cannot sustain a connection.

What does a relationship rooted in difference look like?[1] Our understanding of relationships is deeply grounded in commonality. Family, clan, tribe, and nation are relationships that are defined by common blood, commitment, ancestry, tradition, ritual, or belief. What is a relationship founded on different experiences, education, tradition, and beliefs defined by? How does it work and how does it survive? These are the central questions of this chapter. There are multiple dimensions to the differences that fuel a collaboration, and they are interconnected. In this chapter, we will examine the personal and interpersonal dimensions of managing a connection with an "Other" who is significantly different in important ways.

Presence, Expression, Acceptance, and Engagement

Focusing on or even energetically including differences can create tension and disagreement. It is not the usual way most of us approach relationships. Very few of us probe our relationships for these conflicts; even though working through differences can be a defining moment for a relationship, an indication to the people involved that the relationship can survive a conflict. I suggest that, for any collaboration to thrive, the differences must be *present*, *expressed*, *accepted*, and *engaged*. This is a special kind of connection, one that involves more than merely "dealing" with differences as they arise. A collaboration must proactively delve into the differences so that the two people can explore territory that is new to both. Collaboration depends on the way difference stimulates creativity. Rather than avoiding differences, collaborative relationships move toward them.

Presence

What does it mean for differences to be *present* in a collaborative relationship? It might be tempting to think that a difference is either present or absent. But when we consider perspectives, backgrounds, authority, training, or expertise, any one of these can be more or less present in a relationship. Take, for example, the academic dean who wants his subordinates to call him by his first name. Does this request make his hierarchical difference less present? It is still present to some extent by virtue of his role and authority, but by asking his direct reports to refer to him by an "informal" name, he is asking for that difference (and all that comes with it) to be minimized. The subordinate might appreciate the informality, but she might feel uncomfortable and confused about what to do. If these two people need to work together to design an administrative decision or policy, the dean's request to minimize the presence of hierarchy could affect the subordinate's contribution and ultimately what the relationship is able to create.

Or consider the example of an engineer who is working with a product manager and is told to "stop thinking like an engineer" and think about the larger picture. The product manager is asking the engineer to make his engineering perspective less present. The request testifies to the fact that the engineer *is* an engineer (and is therefore present as such) but simultaneously asks that this aspect of what the engineer brings to the collaboration be toned down (less present in their conversation). We may understand why the product manager makes this request, perhaps she is frustrated by their inability to agree on something that involves both of their areas of expertise; but this request to be less present will have consequences for their work together, especially if the engineer acquiesces to the product manager.

Being present means that the differences in a relationship, those that contribute to the collaboration, are both accessible to and discussable by the two people involved. When a difference is accessible and discussable both people feel able to inquire about the ways in which this difference is affecting their joint work. The difference sits publicly and comfortably alongside the collaborators when they work. Two legislators, a Democrat and a Republican, sitting together to craft a compromise bill, must be able to talk about their differences at every step or their project is doomed. A salesperson and a tech designer must be able to bring their different perspectives to a product strategy conversation or the strategy will suffer from the over-presence or under-presence of their respective contributions. Fears of tension, conflict, or rejection can cause a person to downplay or even hide a different perspective from their collaborator. In the face of these fears, the requirement that differences be present can be a significant challenge.

Expression

There is a distinction between a difference being present and being expressed. For collaborative work, once the key differences are present, they need to be expressed to be enlisted in the creative process. Alderfer described the fullness of this expression between two people as mutuality,[2,3] the extent to which two people are willing and able to express what they think and feel, positive and negative about the shared task before them. Implicit in Alderfer's definition of mutuality are the sources of what we think and feel, the differences in training, background, perspective, and experience. The connection in a collaboration invites that expression, explicitly and literally. Instead of "What do you think?" a librettist collaborating with a composer might ask, "How do you imagine these words can best be set to music? What problems do you foresee? Any changes you would recommend when thinking about the music alone?" These questions actively invite the collaborator to give voice to her perspective and signal that a different point of view is desired at this stage of the collaboration.

When power differences exist in the collaborative relationship, and they almost always do, expressing a point of view or a strongly held opinion can be difficult. This is true even when that view or opinion is sought by the higher power person. Power differences amplify the fears that threaten honest expression of thought or feeling. The lower power collaborator, the person whose "differences" are accorded lower status by their organization or society, may feel that any disagreement with their collaborator can lead to unwanted, negative consequences including the end of the collaboration or of their employment. The higher-power collaborator has the authority or capacity to decide the future of the relationship. In addition, the success or failure of the collaboration has less impact on the higher-power person because of the security of their relative power position. All of which may contribute to the low power collaborator feeling vulnerable. This vulnerability can lead to differences remaining unexpressed.

The higher power collaborator may feel that giving full expression to his opinions will shut down his lower power partner. This feeling may be warranted since power differences themselves, not the words or phrases used, often suppress the expression of conflicting views from "below." In response to this concern, higher-power collaborators may suppress *their* thoughts and feelings, setting off a cycle in which both collaborators are being cautious about what they say. In a classic attempt at collaboration across hierarchical differences, a supervisor asks her direct report about an issue, topic, or problem to be solved. The direct report, concerned about the consequences of disappointing or not satisfying his supervisor (a concern born of the structural vulnerability inherent in power differences) asks the supervisor what she thinks. The supervisor, genuinely wanting to solicit the perspective of the direct report, reiterates a desire to hear from her subordinate. But again, the vulnerability felt by the direct report leads him to ask again, "What do you think?" When, inevitably, the supervisor, trying to be transparent and not wanting to prolong the unproductive exchange says, "How about we try this ...?" the direct report sighs inwardly and wonders to himself why the supervisor didn't just say this in the first place!

Acceptance

The reaction from a collaborator that is probably most feared is rejection. A difference (of opinion, viewpoint, understanding, or judgment) that is rejected, in the form of an eye roll or a vigorous critique, can have lasting effects. Much like touching a hot stove, it only takes one event for us to learn to avoid the pain. Similarly, with rejection, it can be hard for relationships to recover, and it can lead one or both collaborators to avoid expressing their opinions.

What does acceptance look like? It is important to distinguish between acceptance and agreement. To accept the perspective of another is not necessarily to agree with it. In fact, in a collaborative relationship, too much agreement between collaborators can limit the value of the connection by sidestepping the implications of meaningful differences. Acceptance involves a genuine "taking in" of the other's views. It can be described as a process of consideration and reflection on the ideas or perspectives being expressed. We know when we fail at acceptance because we do not pause when hearing the other but instead find ourselves constructing our response before the other has finished their thought or feeling. But failing at acceptance is not rejection, it is rather a failure to practice what Rogers referred to as "active listening,"[4] the practice of taking in the other's words without the interference of one's own thoughts and reactions. It is called a practice because it is not a natural response for most of us and we all fail at it quite regularly. Suspending our own reactions and judgments, for even a few seconds, is one of the most difficult relational skills. The acceptance conveyed by deep listening establishes a connection through which collaborators can build on each other's ways of thinking, seeing, understanding, and imagining.

Engagement

When different perspectives are brought to a relationship, expressed, and taken in by the people involved, the remaining feature of the collaborative connection is the capacity of each person to engage this perspective. Even when an unfamiliar, uncomfortable, or unwelcome opinion has been presented, expressed, and accepted it can still be a struggle to fully engage it. If one collaborator has never been exposed to the perspective of the other, the unfamiliarity of what is being presented can make engagement difficult. Where do I begin? What do I need to understand (that I do not yet understand) to talk about this idea? Have I encountered the idea already and rejected it in the past? If so, that prior rejection, even if I have worked hard to accept the idea in the present can make genuine engagement hard.

I must now take seriously something I have previously discarded. Engaging the different or conflicting ideas of a collaborator means developing a stake in that idea. As the word implies (and the root of the word engage is in the word for pledge or stake), engagement means that you have skin in the game. Standing apart from an idea, acknowledging it, acquiescing to it, or tolerating it is not engaging it.

The challenge is to engage a collaborator's difference without demeaning or dismissing it. Unlike rejection, subtly denigrating another's idea is an ever-present risk in a collaboration because we each enter these relationships with strongly held and developed competencies and perspectives. Our investment in what we do and how we think is what we bring to the collaboration. Engaging a different set of competencies often means suspending our attachment to what makes us valuable to the relationship. It can mean, ironically, disengaging from our own training and background to engage the perspective of the other. Anthropologists, sociologists, and even poets describe a similar process when characterizing the ability to deeply observe a new setting as "making the familiar strange,"[5] the capacity to simultaneously be deeply embedded in a tradition or perspective (or theory) and be genuinely curious about a different one. The curiosity leads to questions aimed at understanding (rather than comparison or judgment). The more deeply we understand the other's perspective, the more potential exists for creative synergy.

The experience of two women in higher education illustrates these four aspects of collaborative connection. Molly and Sabrina (their names have been changed) undertook to create a program on belonging and inclusiveness on their college campus. Molly was a White woman with a senior administrative role. Sabrina was a Black woman faculty member at the college. Collaborating to design and implement a program aimed at the entire college population was a daunting but compelling challenge that both were eager to tackle. It required these two women to form a connection across their major axes of difference. Their struggle, ultimately successful, involved the four elements of collaborative connection and the challenges inherent in each. Some of their differences were *present* because they were rooted in their respective group memberships (e.g., Black and White, faculty and administration) but others were not so easily discerned (e.g., degree of historical sensitivity). Even when present, the two encountered difficulty fully *expressing* how these differences influenced their view of the shared task because of the worries about how the other might react (e.g., fears of angering the other or ruining the relationship) and the implications of these reactions. Molly and Sabrina also struggled to *accept* each other's thoughts and experiences despite their deep commitment to hearing from each other. Sometimes acceptance felt like it required them to give up their own perspective. Engagement, ironically, came easier to them once expression and acceptance had occurred. They worked hard at soliciting the other's views, though this often followed a misunderstanding, conflict, or bruised feelings.

The Role of Individual Limitations

In the previous chapter, our discussion of complementarity touched briefly on the role of individual limitations in the collaborative relationship. My limitations make complementarity possible. In this regard, chemical compounds, formed by the chemical bonding of two or more elements, are a useful metaphor for a collaborative connection. The capacity for two or more elements to form a bond is based on the incompleteness of each element's outer electron ring. (Bear with me!) Noble gases, for example, have complete outer rings (no "holes" that need filling, no capacity to accept or share electrons from another element). As a result, under most conditions these gases cannot form a connection with any other element, they are inert. This characteristic, being inert, can be useful (when, e.g., you want to keep a fruit from rotting for as long as possible, the introduction of an inert gas can retard the oxidation process) but it precludes bonds that create new molecules. Elements that are incomplete have much more chemical potential than elements that are complete unto themselves. And while an inert gas can function very well in one or two ways, connected molecules (chemical compounds) tend to have many more uses.

Individuals who are "complete" or think they are "complete," who behave as if they have no limitations or "weaknesses," will have difficulty forming collaborative connections with others. They may make significant contributions as individuals, but their capacity to be in relationships that create will be limited. Like chemical elements, it is human incompleteness or imperfection that creates the conditions for collaboration. When someone "bonds" with us through the complementarity of their strengths and our limitations, the results can be new and useful (the core elements of creativity). Sodium and chloride, neither of which we would use to season or preserve our food, bond to form common table salt, a compound with innumerable uses.

For the individual collaborator, a relationship with someone whose strengths complement one's own weaknesses or limitations can present both psychological and societal challenges. Most of us subscribe to the belief that all humans have weaknesses and limitations relative to others. We have argued that the presence of these differences in strengths and weaknesses provides the raw material for collaborative relationships. But most of us are also uncomfortable with some of the consequences of this reality. One source of discomfort is the belief that weakness makes us vulnerable, a belief that in some circumstances turns out to be accurate.

Another discomfort is the feeling that weakness or limitation is shameful, a sign of inadequacy or wrongdoing.

When our weaknesses make us feel vulnerable or inadequate, we may choose to try to overcome or "eliminate" them. This only works to a limited extent. No matter how hard we work to turn our weaknesses into strengths, learn what we do not know, and practice a skill until it is well honed, we each retain *relative* strengths and weaknesses. With respect to ourselves, we're better at some things than others, and with respect to other people, most of us know someone who is better at everything we do. Perhaps just as important, we are likely to retain a sense of vulnerability since it is the *knowledge* of our weaknesses that creates the sense of vulnerability and inadequacy.

Our response to feeling shame about our weaknesses is often less about correcting or eliminating them and more about hiding the unwanted piece of who we are. Removing all our weaknesses would be like eliminating the bottom 10% of a distribution. It is, by definition (in this case the definition of being human) impossible. Attempts can be made, however, to hide or deny a weakness. Hiding a limitation is an attempt to make sure that no one can see it. We cover it up or learn to compensate for it, so no one notices. As a young boy who needed glasses, I was unable to recognize faces at a distance. I was ashamed of my inability to recognize friends at a reasonable distance (when everyone else could) so I learned to identify gross patterns in the way people dressed or walked. My coping mechanism (gross pattern recognition) allowed me to hide my limitations. It also prevented me from telling my parents that I couldn't see, a choice that delayed solving the problem.

Instead of hiding a limitation in the face of shameful feelings, we can deny the limitation altogether. The process of denying our weaknesses has the potential "benefit" of hiding the limitation from ourselves as well as others and the feelings of vulnerability that come with it. Unlike most attempts at hiding a limitation, denial is often an unconscious process, a choice we make in the face of our vulnerability, that is out of our awareness. Denial wouldn't work, it wouldn't protect us from the feelings of vulnerability or shame, if we were aware of what we were doing. We believe our denials precisely because we need to think they are true to feel better about ourselves. Something hidden can be revealed (an eye test made real my near-sightedness). A denial is much more resistant to acceptance ("I'm not going to the eye doctor because there is nothing wrong with my eyesight!").

The Shadow

Jung wrote about the *shadow*, the hidden, unacknowledged, inferior aspects of the self.[6] The shadow is the repository of these aspects, a psychological closet without light that holds our unwanted thoughts and feelings.

We treat the shadow as if it were a story (about the self) that can never be told. If it were to be taken into the light of day, it would damage not only how the world sees us (our imperfections, our limitations, our strange habits) but also how we see ourselves. Most of the time we do not even know the closet exists nor what is in it. Locked away in the basement of our unconscious, we hope no one (including ourselves) finds these secrets.

The shadow escapes the closet through misdirection and stealth. We see it, indirectly, in the aspects of others that remind us of ourselves. Seeing it in the other preserves our denial, allowing the unwanted aspect to remain hidden from our harsh judgment. But since the shadow represents the unwanted aspects of the self, the negative feelings associated with these unwanted aspects remain with us. When we see someone in the world who also represents these aspects, we are prone to feel about this other person the way we feel about the unwanted aspects of ourselves, harshly judgmental. This is the process of projective identification.[7] We see in the other what we cannot accept in ourselves and then visit upon this other the feelings, usually critical and rejecting, that we have for this part of ourselves. Most of us encounter this phenomenon often. I believe that using turn signals increases safety on the roads, but I am often too lazy or simply forgetful to use mine. I don't like this hypocrisy about myself, but I am in denial about being a hypocrite until my daughter points out that I rail against others for failing to do what I often fail to do.

In collaborative relationships in which the complementary differences need to be present and expressed, the potential for the projection of our negative feelings about our limitations onto our collaborative partner's strengths is always alive. If, in some ways, the limitations of the other mirror our own, we may project our self-criticism onto the other, complaining about a characteristic, opinion, or passion in *them* that we demean in ourselves.[8] Similarly, but more damaging for collaborations, the *strengths* of the other may remind us of our own weaknesses. When this happens, as it will in almost all collaborations, we may demean the other's strengths to manage our own self-criticism. When I am in the car with someone who dutifully uses their turn signal, I may find myself silently chastising them. Why bother, no one pays attention to turn signals anyway. There isn't anyone within ten car lengths, who are you signaling to?

The implications for collaborative relationships of the internal struggle with our limitations and weaknesses are that these relationships work better to the extent that each collaborator has been able to accept their limitations. Jung referred to this as the assimilation of the shadow,[9] a conscious acceptance rather than an unconscious rejection of what we do not like about ourselves. For most of us, this struggle to accept that which we detest about ourselves is a lifelong endeavor. We are only partially successful at any point in time. But for collaborations, the capacity of each of us to assimilate our own shadow is a core element of the connection we can establish. When I laugh at my daughter's admonition that I am berating the *other* driver for *my* failure to signal, the acceptance allows two things to happen: (1) I increase my odds of using my turn signal the next time because I am on friendly (rather than conflictful) terms with my (occasionally!) irresponsible behavior and (2) my relationship with my daughter is preserved or enhanced because I do not have to defend myself against my self-criticism voiced through her observation.

One final thought on this struggle for self-acceptance. In addition to the psychological forces that make it difficult to identify and accept our limitations, the social world in which we live and work compounds this difficulty. We learn early that when a letter of recommendation asks for strengths and weaknesses, the weaknesses will be amplified and often used as a reason to dismiss the applicant. When we compose a resume, we rarely include anything about our areas of weakness even though we all have them, and our job performance will be enhanced by our awareness of these weaknesses. And those of us who have received formal feedback in our jobs will often leaf through a feedback report (compiled from supervisors, peers, and direct reports) that begins with our strengths and then moves on to our *areas for improvement*. The word "weakness" or "limitation" is rarely used. The implications are clear. If you have any weaknesses, they should be eliminated. If they cannot be eliminated, they should be hidden. Rarely does the world around us, especially the work world, encourage us to accept *both* our strengths and weaknesses and to make a connection with a collaborator to complement the latter.

It is a paradox that our insufficiencies make collaboration possible, yet no one wants to have any insufficiencies! And few would admit that they desire to be in a collaborative relationship with someone who has insufficiencies. Isn't it preferable to have a collaborator with no limitations? The paradox of collaboration strongly suggests the opposite. The key to a collaborative connection is the presence rather than the absence of limitations. Only when our limitations are present can the strengths of our collaborator make a meaningful contribution to our joint work.

An Intimate Relationship

It now becomes apparent that a working collaboration is an intimate relationship. Close relationships tend to be those in which both people are genuinely known to each other. The more intimate the relationship, the less is hidden from the other. Our first intimate relationships are with family members. Living with others 24 hours a day means that it is impossible to hide ourselves from others, even if we have the impulse to do so. We may not like ourselves when we lash out at our mother, but she sees it, as do the others in the family who are present when it happens. When we leave the family, if we have roommates or partners, the possibility (or inevitability!) of being known is once again real. These people see us when we are vulnerable, physically and psychologically. They see us when we are happy and sad, grumpy, and generous. These relationships often last a lifetime in part because we were fully known to and accepted by each other during this period of our lives. As adults, many of our relationships are role-related (job, hobby, volunteer work) and in these relationships, we present only parts of ourselves. We bring eight hours of our "work self" to the job and two hours of our "workout self" to our fitness routine. As a result, most of our relationships are "partial." The sense of being fully known is less present in our adult relationships. Outside of the few 24/7 relationships we have, most of the people in our lives see only what we show them.

Working collaborations are intimate albeit in a restricted way. When two people share a task, bring complementary differences to the work, and need to leverage these differences in the service of their joint creativity, they need to know each other's strengths and weaknesses. As we have discussed, hiding our differences can imperil the success of the collaboration. Being hidden to the other or choosing silence when faced with conflict or difference, reduces the opportunities for creativity. But to be known, fully, even in this restricted way, can be scary as well as creatively satisfying. Being known by someone else involves voluntarily or involuntarily revealing some of the shadow aspects of the self. What if these aspects are rejected by our collaborator? Not unsurprisingly, the depth of our differences is directly related to the depth of our fear of rejection. The more we feel and express our most meaningful difference with our collaborative partner, the more likely we are to fear that these ideas or perspectives will be rejected. And yet, the more we express these differences, the more likely creative work will occur.

Here are two examples of the impact of having one's limitations known to a collaborator. Jenny (the athletic coach) remembers the evolution of her relationship with Tony this way, "As I got to know him, I realized that what he gave off in public wasn't all there was. He was willing to reveal *[to me]* his insecurities, to be honest."[10] The result, for Jenny, was a solidification of the connection between the two colleagues. When I have taught about the relationship between people in leadership roles and those in followership roles, I always ask the participants two questions. First question: Have you ever worked for someone who disclosed a weakness to you, a genuine weakness that required a complementary strength in you to get a job done? Most people, though not all, answer yes to this question. Second question: Did you feel more or less connected to that person after this disclosure? With almost no exceptions, the people who had experienced a weakness in their boss felt more connected to them. We should take note that in both examples, it was not merely the disclosure of a weakness but the capacity of the collaborator to complement the weakness that enhanced the (hierarchical) collaboration. Both the disclosure and the complementarity were necessary. Neither alone was sufficient.[11]

Being known also brings with it obligation. If I do not know that you are worried about how I will react to your idea, if I am unaware of your "insecurity" about the idea (insecurity that is often rooted in your fear of my reaction), then I have no responsibility to take those feelings into account in the way I respond. But once you do reveal your fears, my responsibility to you changes. Knowing your vulnerabilities will, and arguably should, influence how I engage your ideas. For the collaboration to succeed, this obligation cannot suppress my reactions or alter the substance of my engagement, but it might change the emotional tenor of my communication because I now know how you feel about bringing this idea to me and to our collaboration. Being known to each other brings the mutual responsibility that characterizes any intimate relationship, the obligation to take care when entrusted with another's full self, warts, and all.

Shifting Subordination

A collaborative relationship, by the nature of the complementary differences, involves a mutual dependency as well. Our definition of a creative connection is based on the collaborators' belief that neither of them could have produced the joint work on their own. They depend on each other and each other's *different* contributions to create. The result is a dynamic shifting of subordination[12] depending on the requirements of the work and the relative strengths and weaknesses of the collaborators. When a designer and a cabinet maker are creating a bespoke mahogany table, the answer to the question of "who's in charge here" will undoubtedly change as they work on the project. Perhaps the initial sketch comes from the designer (with the cabinetmaker stepping back). When the cabinetmaker weighs in on how the wood will behave or on the structural integrity of the design, it may be the designer's turn to step back. But each of these steps back is temporary. The collaborative work depends on each stepping forward *and* back, alternating strong expression of what they know with equally strong acceptance (and engagement) with what the other knows.

This shifting subordination is not always smooth. Engagement can look and feel like conflict. Stepping back can appear to be resignation or withdrawal. Sometimes there is conflict. Subordinating oneself is rarely easy, especially if one has strongly held opinions based on a lifetime of experience and much individual success. But this is the challenge of shifting subordination, how to allow oneself to be led by another without surrendering the responsibility to engage this (temporary) act of leadership and ultimately to assert one's own. And to meet this challenge embedded in the swirl of emotions that attend leadership and followership in any collaboration.

It can be argued that the two essential components of the collaborative connection are the capacity to elicit and engage the differences brought by the collaborators to the working relationship and the ability to manage the emotions stirred up by the intimate, mutually vulnerable, and interdependent nature of this relationship. In many collaborations, developing the capacity to elicit and engage difference is easier than managing the emotions that come with it. This makes intuitive sense since the differences are often what brought the relationship together and sustain its creative potential. When we think of collaborations, it is the connection across differences that comes to mind. We rarely think of the range of emotions that ebb and flow in a collaboration. Even more rare is a thought about how these emotions might be managed in the service of the collaboration itself.

The ability to manage strong emotions in a relationship has been described as the capacity of the relationship to serve as a container for the feelings that arise during the work.[13] The key to this way of conceptualizing a collaborative relationship is the observation that when the emotions of collaborative work "leak out" of the relationship, the vitality of the collaboration is jeopardized. If, for example, I take my frustrations with not being heard by my collaborator to someone outside the relationship, this reduces the urgency or need to express this feeling inside the relationship. Not hearing my frustration, my collaborator may continue to act in a way that leads me to feel unheard. Ultimately, I might conclude that I'm not making much of a contribution and leave the relationship. Similarly, if I take my appreciation for your contributions to someone else, raving about your insight or skill to a friend or partner but do not express those feelings directly to you, I may one day find that you have left the relationship because you did not feel that your contributions were valued by me.

Functioning as a container means that the collaborators, over time, come to trust that the expression of their emotions, their competitive feelings, envy, conflicting thoughts, passionate objections as well as their appreciation, admiration, and gratitude will not destroy the bonds (the commitment to the work and to each other) that connect them. This trust is built incrementally over time. Each person, tentatively at first, puts out a feeling and pays close attention to how the other reacts. If the reaction demonstrates that the feeling can be a part of the relationship and need not be kept out or suppressed, the containing function of the relationship is enhanced. If not, the container is weakened, increasing the chances that this feeling will be taken out of the relationship. This process of building the containing capacity of the relationship, even when it works, has the flavor of taking two steps forward and one step back. Such is the reality of trust building, the process of coming to believe that the other will not exploit one's own emotions or vulnerabilities.[14] As long as a collaborative relationship can contain the emotional currents of joint collaborative work, creative connection is possible.

Endnotes

1 Kenwyn K. Smith and David N. Berg, 'Cross Cultural Groups at Work,' *European Journal of Management* 15, no. 1 (1997): 8–15.
2 Clayton P. Alderfer, Robert Kaplan, and Kenwyn K. Smith, 'The Effect of Variations in Relatedness Need Satisfaction on Relatedness Desires,' *Administrative Science Quarterly* 19 (1974): 507–532.
3 Carl Rogers, *On Becoming a Person* (Boston: Houghton Mifflin, 1961).
4 Carl Rogers, *Client-Centered Therapy* (Boston: Houghton Mifflin, 1951).
5 Clifford Geertz, *The Interpretation of Cultures* (New York: Basic Books, 1973).
6 Carl G. Jung, *Collected Works*, Vol. 9 (Princeton: Princeton University Press, 1970).
7 Melanie Klein, 'Notes on Schizoid Phenomena,' *International Journal of Psychoanalysis* 27 (1946): 99–110.
8 Leroy Wells, Jr., The Group-as-a-Whole Perspective and its Theoretical Roots, in Arthur D. Coleman and Marvin H. Geller (Eds.) *Group Relations Reader,* Vol. 2 (Washington, D.C.: A. K. Rice Institute, 1985), pp. 109–126.
9 Carl G. Jung, *Collected Works*, Vol. 9 (Princeton: Princeton University Press, 1970).
10 Personal Interview.
11 David Berg, Resurrecting the Muse: Followership in Organizations, in Edward Klein, Faith Gabelnick, Peter Herr (Eds.), *Psychodynamics of Leadership* (Madison, CT: Psychosocial Press, 1998).
12 David Berg, Resurrecting the Muse: Followership in Organizations, in Edward Klein, Faith Gabelnick, Peter Herr (Eds.), *Psychodynamics of Leadership* (Madison, CT: Psychosocial Press, 1998).
13 William Kahn, *Holding Fast: The Struggle for Mental Health* (New York: HarperCollins, 2003).
14 Lauren Taylor and David N. Berg, 'The Challenge of Mutual Disclosure in Global Health Partnerships,' *Perspectives in Biology and Medicine* 62 no. 4 (2019): 657–673.

Chapter 6

Falling Together

Earlier in this book we explored the roots of the word collaboration. Unsurprisingly, one of the components is *labore* which, when combined with "co" becomes working together. We also learned that *labore* has its roots in the experience of slipping or struggling or falling. Working together conveys struggling together or even falling together. When two people carry their differences into the collaborative relationship, they struggle with the weight of the task. If they are successful in creating something from their efforts, they struggle at times to manage the weight of their differences. A collaboration struggles with both the weight of the work and the weight of the differences necessary to produce the work. What causes two people to slip, struggle, or fall together in the first place, to carry the weight together rather than toil alone?

Falling together is a gravitational experience. When we walk, our foot falls together with the ground. Walking is a series of falls. We step out and our foot falls to the ground. To take the next step, we must pry our foot from the ground, for having fallen together with the earth, our foot would stay there were it not for the strength of our muscle pulling it away. If gravity did not pull our legs down, walking would be much harder if not impossible. Falling is about being pulled together as Newton famously observed. When two people collaborate, they are most often brought together by a gravitational pull that causes them to fall together. As we now know, the etymology of the word suggests that the line between falling together (to work together) and collapsing (under the weight of that work) is a thin one. Without falling together, however, there is no collaboration.

The most common force pulling people to work together is necessity or crisis. Two people need each other to accomplish an objective. In the case of collaboration, the need is more than just labor, it is the need for the other's complementary skills, background, or perspective. This need often forces people together. In organizations, this force can be supplied by the institution itself. Two people from different departments, for example, are assigned to come up with a plan that requires substantive input from

DOI: 10.4324/9781032701998-6

both functional perspectives. The force can also be supplied by the task at hand. Creating an opera requires both a librettist and a composer, for each of these professional activities often prohibits one person from possessing both sets of skills. As a result, the job of producing an opera drives poets and musicians together. The story of Apollo 13 involves numerous collaborations spawned by the challenge to bring the wounded spaceship and its occupants safely to Earth.

Gabrielle Zevin's book *Tomorrow and Tomorrow and Tomorrow* is the fictional story of Sadie and Sam, two video game designers who met as young adults, created video games together, and (mostly) sustained a collaboration over two decades. I write "mostly" because their fictional relationship looks a lot like the real ones described in this book, a tribute to Zevin's understanding of collaboration. Near the end of the novel, Sadie reflects on her relationship with Sam and her awareness that their accomplishment had required the two of them.

> Would Sadie have been the designer she became without Sam's ambition for them? The work had been hers, yes, but it had equally been his. It had been theirs, and it wouldn't have existed without both of them. This was a tautology that had only taken her the better part of two decades to understand.[1]

Opportunity for mutual benefit can also pull people together, especially when the benefit cannot be achieved by either person alone. An inventor needs a business plan to realize the economic value of an invention. A businessperson needs a worthy product to have a shot at economic success. A case in point. Julee Rosso and Sheila Lukins met when Julee hired Sheila to cater an event for her in New York City in the late 1970s. Julee had recently started her own consultancy business in marketing and promotion in the fashion industry. Sheila, the caterer, was also new to her business though not new to cooking having been trained at the Cordon Bleu School in London. Julee enjoyed cooking and good food. She was impressed with the creativity and quality of Sheila's food and pitched Sheila the idea of setting up their own gourmet take-out food restaurant in the city. After some thought, Sheila agreed, and the foundation of The Silver Palate was put in place. The restaurant was very successful, creating uniquely seasoned foods, sauces, and prepared dishes. The restaurant grew into a preserved food business and eventually a gift catalog from which their prepared foods could be ordered. When they published *The Silver Palate Cookbook*, the business took off as did their notoriety in the food industry.[2]

Sometimes, more often than we realize, the force that pulls people together to collaborate originates in the relationship between the two people themselves. Rather than the collaboration occurring in response to some external forces, these collaborations are an expression of a falling together that has already occurred. Two artists who respect each other's work decide to work together on a project because the work promises to make concrete what the two people feel, the potential latent in their relationship. Most often seen in the artistic world, but also prevalent in business, sports, and science these collaborations can be initially formed without a specific task. They are relationships in search of a task to give expression to the creativity that the two people involved feel when they work together. Examples abound. Two athletes who decide to play on the same team because of how they play together. Two academics who find that their first conversation about their overlapping interests lasts for hours. Two serial entrepreneurs who, aware of each other's accomplishments, have long desired to work on a project together.

Smith and I had been drawn to each other since graduate school. We had developed a deep friendship around shared interests and hardships. We had traveled together and played together. (I taught him poker and baseball; he taught me Risk and rugby.) Although we were in the same field, we had never worked together. One day we looked at each other and said, almost simultaneously, "Let's write something together." Then began the search for a topic and an approach. Our relationship drove the search for a task.

Whether pulled together by necessity, mutual interest, institutional need, or the nascent potential of a relationship, many collaborators describe their attraction to each other as a critical component of their success. Gravity is the attraction of two bodies to each other. Through this lens, falling together is a process of mutual attraction. We fall in love because we are, for one reason or another, attracted to the other person. We "fell in with a particular crowd" because of mutual attraction. The language of becoming a relationship is filled with gravitational images of being drawn together, falling for each other, or being unable to resist the pull of the other. Pablo Picasso and Georges Braque were artists who were introduced to each other in 1910 in Paris. This introduction began a collaboration that gave birth to the Cubist movement in art. As Emily Bardack Kies writes, "It is unlikely that Cubism as we know it could have developed without the interaction that arose between *[Picasso and Braque]* which was at its most intense during 1910–1912." Picasso himself described this period in language reminiscent of the early stages of falling in love, "Almost every evening either I went to Braque's studio or Braque came to mine. Each of us *had* to see what the other had done during the day."[3]

Even in relationships that are mandated by an organization (a project team, a police partnership, movie co-stars), the success of the relationship, its capacity to do more than merely exist, depends on finding some dimension of connection or attraction, some appreciation of what the other brings to the work. The actress Emily Blunt in an interview about romantic scenes she hated doing talked about the need to find something in the other actor, even a small thing, that she could appreciate to provide the chemistry needed to create a compelling piece of work.[4] Chemistry is another way of describing an attraction, a bond that forms the basis for something joint and new.

Attraction and Intimacy

The intense attraction at the outset of a collaboration often leads to an intimacy that sustains the relationship through its work. As we have noted, intimate relationships are ones in which both parties know and are known by the other. Our daily lives are a series of partial exposures. We express some parts of ourselves in some settings and hold back other parts that we deem inappropriate or unnecessary. We can be embarrassed when a part of ourselves that is only expressed in one part of our life, comes out in another. Our competitive, fighting spirit normally given free rein on the playing field comes out in a card game with an eight-year-old. The insecurities we divulge to our life partner leak out to a stranger after a few alcoholic drinks on a 12-hour layover in the airport. The more intimate a relationship is the more parts of us are known to the other person. If a disclosure causes the other person to back away from the relationship, the level of intimacy is capped by that disclosure. The more a relationship continues in the face of increasingly full disclosure, the more intimate the relationship feels.

The safety of being known more fully creates the conditions for creative connection. I no longer worry about being seen as crazy or being rejected for my thoughts and feelings. As a result, I feel freer to offer them to the perspective of the other person who then, in turn, feels free to give expression to their reactions. This is not always the case. Most of us are not ever free of the anxieties that attend being known. But the closer we come to this intimate connection, the more a relationship can work with what each person brings to the task. Intimacy also helps the relationship contain the emotions stirred by the differences in a collaboration. I have argued that these differences are the raw material for the creative process. But these same differences are a source of tension and conflict. The intimacy of a collaboration helps two people through the tensions. When we know what triggers the other or we know how important a facet of their identity is to them, we may not flee the relationship when these differences show up. We may not embrace them, but we are more likely to hang around until the storm between us passes.

When two people come together and form a bond that enables creative work across their differences and can sustain that work by their intimate knowledge and ultimate acceptance of each other, they can also serve different functions for each other. Distinct from their individual skills and talents, and from the group-based experience and expertise they bring, collaborative relationships also benefit from what each person does for the other. Two people with different and complementary characteristics are not enough to make a collaboration. We have referred to these differences as ingredients in the creative recipe. Are they shaken, stirred, sifted, grated, or blended? Are they baked, broiled, sautéed, grilled, or poached? How are these different elements combined, and what roles do each of the two people play in this process? The capacity for another to play a role in the creative relationship provides a pull, an attraction that not only initiates but also sustains the collaboration.

Supporting Roles

The most important role that collaborators play for each other is the *complement*. As we have described it, the complementary "other" fills in gaps in experience and expertise and by doing so makes possible the creation of something unique to the two individuals involved. A complement is not simply a different "other" but rather one whose strengths combine with our limitations to produce something "whole" and new. Remember the sodium atom? It is different in atomic structure from nitrogen, but they do not combine well. Putting them together creates nothing. Sodium and chlorine atoms on the other hand combine easily and well, creating common table salt, a molecule born of the chemical bond between two complementary elements. Like chemical elements, people can provide a complement to more than one other person. The essence of serving a complementary role in a collaboration is that what each person contributes to the process is needed to create the final product. And unlike some of the roles discussed below, the complementary role is usually symmetrical, each person adds something to the relationship that is missing in the other.

Collaborators also serve as each other's *muse*, the other who stimulates our own creativity. Like the complement, the muse is necessary for the creative process. Without a muse, the creativity latent in the individual is unrealized or unexpressed and therefore unavailable to the collaboration. Collaborators describe their relationship with each other in terms that evoke the role of muse. Maurice Sendak, an illustrator, children's book author, and set designer described his relationship with Mozart as a collaboration. Mozart, through his music, inspired Sendak's creativity. He put it this way, "When Mozart is playing in my room, I am in conjunction with something I can't explain.... I don't need to. I know that if there's a purpose for life, it was for me to hear Mozart."[5] When we talk about being stimulated by the thoughts or questions of another, we are invoking the role of a muse. When a collaborator says or does something that opens a door to our own thinking, a door that we didn't know existed and could never have walked through, they are functioning as a muse. The verb form of the word also plays a role in the collaborative process. Collaborators often muse together, and mull over a problem or an idea in ways that neither would have or could have alone. The musing process itself stimulates the relationship, suggesting paths that might have been unexplored by each person alone.

Sadie (the fictional video game developer) described Sam's role in her life in a way that underscored the intimacy that forms the foundation of the muse function. Observing the collaboration between two other game developers, Sadie reflects on her relationship with Sam.

> She liked Simon and Ant. How could she not like them? They reminded her of Sam and herself … a difference was that Ant and Simon were lovers. She would watch them and feel a touch of … envy at their intimacy. She wondered what it would have been like if she and Sam had been lovers. And in the end, she had decided she preferred being his creative partner to his lover. There were so many people who could be your lover, but, if she were honest with herself, there were relatively few people who could move you creatively.[6]

The *catalyst* is another role played by a collaborator. A catalyst precipitates a process or an event. Unlike a compliment, more like a muse, the catalyst makes something happen. In some cases, the catalyst enables something within their partner, initiating a reaction that otherwise would not have occurred. In other cases, it is a reaction within the collaboration that is ignited by the catalyst. Though there is much overlap between the role of muse and catalyst, the catalyst is less a part of the creative outcome. The catalytic role, at that moment, is concerned with jump-starting the creative process in the other collaborator or in the relationship. If someone says, "Let's go for a walk just to change the scenery and to see what happens," they are functioning as a catalyst. A muse, in contrast, might say "Have you ever thought of using the light through the trees as a metaphor for insight?" and would engage the conversation that ensued to aid in its development. We cannot digest certain foods without enzymes, the catalysts for the digestive process. But the enzyme is not a part of the nutrition that it helps create. Its function is to facilitate a process.

Smith would often function as a catalyst in our relationship. His questions would cause me to think outside the familiar contours of my mind. I would often pause before responding to Smith's questions (not something I regularly did when asked a question!) because the question opened an area of inquiry that I had not realized was within me. One example: when we were writing about intergroup relations Smith once asked, "What was the primal intergroup?" I was stunned. He was referring to Freud's metaphorical theory of the "primal horde," the hypothetical first group of humans. What, Smith was asking, was the primal intergroup, the first or paradigmatic example of relations between groups? My mind took flight (as did his), catalyzed by his question. Bundini Brown seems to function as a muse with respect to Mohammed Ali's rhetorical gifts, stimulating and contributing to Ali's creativity. But with respect to his boxing, the motivation he provided Ali, coaxing and then igniting the champion's talents, seemed catalytic.[7]

The final role takes this facilitation function to its logical next step. The *midwife's* role brings out the creativity of the collaborative partner. The midwife's *role* neither stimulates nor precipitates, it aids in the delivery of the creative product. When describing the midwife function, it is especially important to keep in mind that this is a role being played by one of the collaborators for the other or for the collaborative relationship. When performing this *role*, one of the collaborators is helping the other give birth to an idea or a solution. At an earlier time in the relationship, this same collaborator might have functioned as a complement, bringing their different strengths to the relationship, or a muse, stimulating creativity in their partner, or a catalyst, precipitating a process of thought or action in the partner. But when the time comes to deliver something, to breathe life into that which has been gestating in their collaborator or in the collaboration, the midwife's role takes the creative connection through a final stage. Hesketh Pearson, in his book on Gilbert and Sullivan, describes Gilbert's role in ways that evoke images of midwifing a birth

> Gilbert was in a very real sense the begetter of Sullivan's best music; he was the Svengali who by hypnotizing Trilby-Sullivan could create the notes he wanted, and Sullivan surrendered gladly to the magnetism of a personality that could extract from him the essence of light-hearted happiness he was otherwise not able to express.[8]

These roles can be played at different times by each of the collaborators, or one collaborator may gravitate toward one or more roles on a regular basis. As with any social system, roles help keep the collaborative relationship together. Once formed by the initial pull of shared need and benefit, the evolution of roles, with each collaborator moving in and out of the various functions, serves to bind the two individuals to the task at hand. The relationship, without the capacity to muse, for example, might struggle to find playful, easy ways to explore both their differences and the complex nature of their work. Without complementary contributions, it might not experience the heat and light that emerge from the clash of different experiences and opinions. Without catalyzing each other to write or think or sculpt or envision, it might never reach the activation energy necessary for the creative process to ignite. And without the steadying hand to deliver a new creation through the pain and effort of the collaborative birth process, the relationship might never realize the fruits of its labor.

A Back Story

There is a back story to the formation of collaborative relationships. This backstory involves the individual work that precedes the falling together and makes the falling together possible. This work is done by each of the collaborators in their own way, but some minimum must be done for collaborative relationships to have a chance of forming. The work involves change in the minds of the collaborators, specifically change in the way each views themselves and the world around them.

Let's start with the world. Earlier in this book I asserted that groups shape us and our perception of the world around us. Our families, communities, friendships, work groups, religion, and cultural heritage all "teach" us about the people and institutions in our environment. Our family has a history with other families that translates into trust or feud, friendship or estrangement, openness or wariness. Similarly, and often even more powerfully, our culture, religion, or nationality includes "information" about other cultures, religions, or nationalities. We learn about other groups – families, cultures, religions – from our own groups long before most of us have direct experience with these other groups. When we do have direct contact with *other* groups, the experience is often interpreted through discussions we have had within our *own* group. By the time we can look for or accept collaborators, we often already have well-developed impressions of the groups to which they belong. We apply those impressions from afar, when watching television or reading stories about these groups. We also apply these impressions in the initial moments, hours, weeks, or even years of our contact with members of these groups.

These impressions or "teachings" are often formed early in our lives and, as a result, live deep below our conscious minds. Even before we can conceptualize groups, before we can understand the complexity of intergroup relations throughout history, we have been given impressions of the groups that surround us. "Don't talk to strangers," for example, is important information for small children *and* it is one of our first lessons about a group called "strangers." Not all the lessons we learn about other groups are fearful or mistrustful. We learn about groups that are to be respected and trusted as well as those that are not.

This is a normal part of our upbringing for it prepares us, for better and for worse, to make our way in the social world. But it is also an error-filled and limiting process. These lessons come with a price. Designed to protect or privilege, we learn only some information about the "other," information that provides only a partial picture of other groups. We know the lived experience of other groups in a very limited way, so what we teach about these groups is similarly limited. If we are teaching about a trustworthy group, we often leave out the warnings. This is the root of the feeling of betrayal, the realization that our understanding of a "trustworthy" group (e.g., teachers, clerics, coaches) was wrong or dangerously incomplete. If we are teaching about groups that we consider untrustworthy, the lesson can be similarly limited or incomplete. Most often when someone says, "You know how they are," the reality is we do not.

There are two powerful implications for forming collaborations contained in the observation that our views of other groups, though not exclusively negative, are both limited and potentially demeaning. When we consider collaborating with someone from another group, a different professional or educational background, a different cultural or national identity, or a different organizational or institutional setting, we must confront our own images of these groups, and we must contend with the images that other members of our group also carry with them. Our individual perceptions as well as the perceptions held by those with whom we share an important (to us) group membership can make the forming of a connection with members of other groups difficult if not inconceivable.

Our membership in a group – a family or community or profession – is often contingent on subscribing to the shared beliefs, practices and norms of the group. These shared beliefs connect us to the group. If our beliefs change or evolve, our connection to our group can weaken. If the group is important to us, if it sustains us in material, emotional, or spiritual ways, we are likely to be cautious in discarding or ignoring the beliefs and practices of the group for fear of weakening a connection that is meaningful. Some of those beliefs and practices involve other groups, beliefs, and practices that in some cases involve regulating our contact and relationships with members of these other groups. The classic example is the prohibition of marrying someone outside of one's group. It is a paradigmatic example of restricting the creative connection across group boundaries. Almost every group has such prohibitions implicit or explicit in the lessons it teaches its members. Whether a religious prohibition about marrying outside the faith or a political warning about "getting in bed" with the other side or a subtle "management" of another professional group inside one's organization, the message is similar. Be wary of the stranger.

As a result, when we consider a collaboration with someone who belongs to different groups, we are likely to confront the lessons we have learned about those groups. If we do not, our chances of connecting are reduced dramatically. Put another way, whenever we observe a collaboration between members of different groups, it is likely that both have had to change what they were taught about the groups to which their collaborator belongs. In 1971, Richard Nixon, then President of the United States, called the president of the American Bar Association (ABA) to the White House. Nixon's political advisors were encouraging him to appoint a woman to the Supreme Court ahead of the 1972 elections to secure more of the women's vote. There had yet to be a female Supreme Court Justice. When asked to recommend some female candidates, a request routinely made to the head of the ABA, he replied that there were no qualified women in the country.[9] Imagine what he, or thousands of other ABA members, might have thought about collaborating with a woman on a trial or a legal article. The lesson (male) lawyers probably learned from their senior professional colleagues was that members of the group "women" were inferior and not appropriate collaborators.

This scenario repeats itself when other groups are substituted, not because human beings are evil but because the lessons we learn about other groups are often historical vestiges kept in place and handed down without revision. Those of us who work in "operations" know how the "finance" people will react to a new proposal. Those of us who work in primary care know how the surgeons will act when they get involved in patient care. Those of us who build houses know how architects work. Our experience with members of these groups influences our perceptions of them, but equally important, at the onset of a potential collaboration, the images of other groups that we have internalized from the "education" we receive from our own groups can inhibit falling together. These images tend to be ethnocentric, emphasizing the positive qualities of our own group and the negative qualities of other groups.[10] They dissuade us from making a connection that might enhance our capacity to create a new song, product, book, curriculum, strategy, opera, script, or understanding. Confronting these images, suspending, if only for a few moments, the "wisdom" of our own groups, makes possible "falling in" with someone from a different group.

The legacy of the education we receive has another implication for the formation of collaborative relationships. Groups transmit their understanding of other groups for several reasons including protecting their own group members from harm, equipping group members with information to aid their decision-making in a world of many groups, and maintaining their "place" in the world – their own autonomy, survival, identity, and resources. When someone from within the group questions or confronts these cultural messages, the group is often mobilized to resist any changes, fearing that changes will have negative consequences for the group. This resistance, in the form of advice, sanction, ostracism, or even punishment can be directed at an individual who reaches out to make a connection across groups because in many cases this attempt to make a relationship is itself a violation of the group's teaching. The more different the group, the greater the "social distance"[11] between the two groups, the greater the communicated consequences. To return to a previous example, a group may teach its "young" not to mingle with (or "marry") someone from another group, but should a person begin to hang around with someone from that other group or become involved with them, the opprobrium often ramps up to include accusations of disloyalty and threats of expulsion. The reactions of *our* group to a relationship with someone from *another* group are a powerful deterrent to the formation of a collaborative relationship.

Organizational authority can also be used to prohibit or facilitate collaboration. The expectation that employees will "go through channels," for example, can lead to a stifling of cross-departmental relationships. This "rule" is often put in place for good reasons but can have the unintended consequence of making cross-departmental boundary crossing more difficult. Similarly, organizational "lore" about the different functional groups in organizations can inhibit creative contact across these groups. Product design people may not involve people from the finance department until they "have their ducks in a row" because "everyone knows" that the "bean counters" will just say no. And while it may be true that the finance function's role in the organization is to evaluate all new initiatives from a (conservative) financial point of view, the effect of this cultural view of the finance department is to dissuade early contact that might lead to creative collaborative solutions. This same dynamic can be seen in organizational views of tech and human relations functions.

Other organizational contextual factors similarly contribute to people not finding each other for creative connections. Collaboration often requires an investment of time and resources. In an organization in which everyone is doing a full-time job, the time that must be found to enable two people to try to create something new can be substantial. Economic pressures can make this hard to authorize. In the absence of formal financial support, people must take their own time to collaborate, putting strain on the rest of their working and non-working lives and reducing the chances that such "off the books" collaborations will occur. Finally, and perhaps most importantly, the reward and promotion practices of most organizations work, often unintentionally, against collaboration across different areas or departments. In most organizations, whether industrial, financial, academic, medical, or legal promotions and rewards are based on success within a given specialty. This emphasis is designed to produce excellence within an area of expertise that, in turn, contributes to organizational reputation and success. But like specialization more broadly, these practices have an impact on people looking outside their areas of expertise for the creative connection that might come from relationships that stretch across areas of expertise. Many organizations espouse "interdisciplinary" or "interdepartmental" collaborations, but few can point to genuine work across areas because their promotional and reward practices keep people working hard within their own areas.

Modern organizations have advanced the efficiency of work, and in many cases its quality, by virtue of increased specialization. The more time a person spends developing their skills and talents *within* an area, the better they become. But this tends to restrict their contact with people from other areas and reduces the odds of falling into a collaborative relationship with someone from these areas. That said, organizations do put policies and practices in place to encourage possible collaborations. Cross-functional teams exist when a problem or opportunity requires different expert contributions. Unfortunately, these forms of collaboration often struggle to make meaningful connections because of the other factors described above. A patient care team may have the necessary and complementary skills to offer comprehensive care, but the implicit hierarchy in a hospital may lead the members to defer to the physician or even to the surgeon (as first among "equals" among physicians).

It is impressive that so many collaborations exist. The odds against forming such a relationship seem long. It can be argued that every collaborative relationship is subversive, undermining the integrity of the groups to which each of us belongs. Many of the lessons and prohibitions we learn *should* dissuade us from collaborating with others and they often do. But just as often people from different backgrounds and diverse groups fall together out of necessity, mutual interest, or benefit, or simply because they like each other. In an odd but compelling way, the desire to collaborate feels like a deep-rooted imperative in human beings. And perhaps that makes sense given collaboration's role in our survival as a species.

Endnotes

1 Gabrielle Zevin, *Tomorrow, and Tomorrow, and Tomorrow* (Knopf, 2022), ISBN 978-0593321201.
2 Mortimer Levitt, *How to Start Your Own Business Without Losing Your Shirt* (New York: Atheneum, 1988).
3 Emily Bardack Kies, *Picasso and Braque: Pioneering Cubism* (Pamphlet: Museum of Modern Art MOMA, 1989–1990).
4 Charlotte Phillipp, Interview with Emily Blunt, *People*, May 6, 2024.
5 Maurice Sendak: 'Where the Wild Things Are' (2004), interview by Bill Moyers, PBS.org.
6 Gabrielle Zevin, *Tomorrow, and Tomorrow, and Tomorrow* (Knopf, 2022), ISBN 978-0593321201.
7 Todd Snyder, *Bundini: Don't Believe the Hype* (Boston Massachusetts: Hamilcar Publications, 2020).
8 Hesketh Pearson, *Gilbert and Sullivan: A Biography* (New York: Harper and Bros, 1935).
9 Renee Knake Jefferson and Hannah Brenner Johnson, *Shortlisted: Women in the Shadows of the Supreme Court* (New York: New York University Press, 2020).
10 Robert A. Levine and Donald T. Campbell, *Ethnocentrism: Theories of Conflict, Ethnic Attitudes, and Group Behavior* (New York: John Wiley and Sons, 1972).
11 Joe C. Magee and Pamela K. Smith. "The Social Distance Theory of Power," *Personality and Social Psychology Review* 17, no. 2 (2013): 158–186.

Chapter 7

Driven Apart

One of the central contentions of this book is that collaborative relationships inevitably fall apart or separate. This separation can be temporary, lasting hours, or days, or weeks. It can be permanent, ending the relationship. No matter the duration or the outcome, separation is a normal and necessary part of any collaboration. The word itself carries the emotional reality that collaboration is difficult and weighty, labor intensive, and liable to collapse. Over the next two chapters, we explore two sets of forces that act on collaborative relationships causing them to come apart. One of these is internal to the relationship itself, driving the collaboration apart. The other comes from outside the relationship pulling at the collaborative bond. This chapter begins with answers to some questions concerning collaborative relationships falling apart. Why is separation not just characteristic of collaborations but necessary? How does it happen? What does collaborative separation look and feel like? It then describes the internal forces that drive the two people out of the collaboration. The next chapter then moves to focus on the external forces that pull collaborative relationships apart.

Most collaborations involve some level of tension. As we have already discussed, the differences that each person brings to the relationship provide the necessary spark for the creative work. This *relational* creative tension is what distinguishes the process of collaborative work from *individual* creative work during which the creative tension is located inside the person. These differences give the collaboration its edge, its strength, and its identity, an identity distinct and separate from the individual identities of the two collaborators. But these same differences threaten the collaboration in several ways. When too much tension is generated by the differences, conflict can paralyze the work and ultimately cause one or both people to move away from the relationship. When there is too little tension in a collaboration, the result is a lack of creative energy brought about by the absence of meaningful differences between the individuals. In the case of too much tension, the individual *differences* push the collaborators apart.

DOI: 10.4324/9781032701998-7

In the case of too little tension, the evolving *sameness* of the collaborators drives them from each other.

When two people, different in significant and important ways, form a collaboration, their differences both stimulate and vex. Anyone who has been in such a relationship who tells you that there is no vexation is hiding some of the truth. David Eden in his book *Gilbert and Sullivan: The Creative Conflict* describes this vexation succinctly: "Essentially Gilbert refused to write words that could not be heard through the music, while Sullivan refused any longer to write music which gave primary consideration to the audibility of the words."[1] It can seem incredible that these two created anything together. And yet, it cannot be any other way. If the other's differences were only stimulating, we might be tempted to adopt or mimic these differences. We would become more like the other and the potential for creative connection would diminish. If the other's difference was only vexing, we would be tempted to either try to change them or to leave them. Again, both approaches to a vexing other remove the possibility of creative connection. If we are successful in changing the other (possible but not easy), we remove the elements in the other that enable creativity. If we leave the relationship, we are no longer vexed, but neither are we in a collaboration any longer.

A relationship that is simultaneously stimulating and vexing, and needs to remain that way, is inherently unstable. Where once quirkiness was attractive and stimulating because it was different from our own way of being, now it grates on us. When an enlightening professional perspective becomes an inflexible demand, we find ourselves dreading another "conversation" because we fear that it will become another lecture. If this occurs in the early stages of the collaboration, the relationship may not survive. The connection that enables a relationship to tolerate or, in the case of a collaboration, benefit from internal (creative) tensions has not yet formed or is not strong enough to hold the two people together.

Frayed Connection

After a collaborative relationship has formed and worked together, there is enough of a bond to maintain the relationship as it encounters these inevitable vexations. At this point in the collaboration the tension around "annoyances" may point to something critical to the survival of the relationship. It is most likely a symptom rather than a cause of a frayed connection. When one or more of the dimensions of connection disappear, the result can be that the differences now rub rather than ignite, burn rather than spark, and inflame rather than inspire. The irritation now drives the collaborators apart as a way of gaining some relief from the conflict between them. It is important to bear in mind that the differences, always present and often functional for the collaboration, now stimulate conflict not because they have become more pronounced or because they have just surfaced, but rather because the relational connection has eroded. The evolved tenuousness of the connection makes the differences problematic where once they were experienced as the lifeblood of the collaboration.

The separation that follows the fraying of the collaborative connection can be a correction, an expression of the need by one or both collaborators to stand back from a relationship that is not working the way they hoped it would. The conflict and the separation convey a frustration with one or more dimensions of the connection. It may be that one person is upset with the other's lack of engagement or lack of acceptance. There can be an imbalance in the level of involvement in the collaboration that leads one person to feel that they are carrying more of the responsibility for the maintenance or logistical work of the relationship. The separation allows the two collaborators to step back and reassess the connection to decide whether they want to continue and if so, what aspects of the connection need to change or be repaired. The separation allows this mutual assessment by taking both people out of the tension and conflict that has highlighted the underlying problem. The conflict both reveals the frayed connection and drives the collaborators into a separation that could enable them to address it. Jenny, the athletic coach with a decades-long collaboration with Tony put it this way, "When we disagreed, if I took it personally and I talked to Tony, he might defend himself or banter in the moment, but he would come back to it, and we would talk. Otherwise, it festers."[2]

Fusion

The other force that drives a collaboration apart occurs when the individual identities are submerged in the collaboration. We described collaborative relationships as intimate because these relationships require the individuals in them to know each other and to be known by each other. Most importantly, it requires each person to bring their flaws as well as their talents, their insecurities, and their confidence into the relationship. The mutual acknowledgment and exploration of both deficits and assets form the basis of a close relationship. It also forms the basis of a relationship that can use and build on these individual strengths and weaknesses. The closeness born of this deepening process of knowing and being known fully can form a bubble around the relationship. The bubble is created by the two people because this feeling of being known fully and of being accepted fully is quite rare. The bubble preserves and protects the collaboration (or any intimate relationship) and the feelings that attend it.

In any intimate relationship, the "oneness" of a close relationship can lead either or both individuals to experience the loss of their individual identity. This loss of identity is not inevitable, but when it happens the result can be less dramatic than when collaborators clash, but the consequences for the relationship can be similar. Years ago, I was asked to be on a panel at a professional society meeting. When it was my turn to speak, the moderator gave a two-minute introduction that began with my name. She told the audience where I worked, my most recent professional publication, and some of my accomplishments. The only thing she got right was my name. Everything else she said was accurate *about my collaborator*! By this point in my life, Smith and I had done a lot of work together and we were known in the field as a collaborative pair. But this was something else. My personal identity, other than my name, had disappeared into the collective identity of the collaboration.

After I gently and respectfully corrected the record, roiling inside at the insult and the humiliation of the erasure, and had given my talk, I realized that it was not simply that I had lost my identity but also that it had been replaced with my collaborator's. I hadn't disappeared into the black hole of the collaboration. I had been replaced by my more well-known partner. When I eventually spoke to Smith about my experience and my feelings of being eclipsed by his accomplishments and reputation, he told me that the same thing had happened to him! It seemed that our relationship, our collaboration, had displaced us both. People now thought of us as "Smith and Berg," one entity. Any sense of who we were as individuals had become lost in the powerful identity of our collaboration. We are not alone in this regard. People confuse Abbot and Costello, Watson and Crick, Rosso and Lukins not because the individuals in any of these pairs are similar in appearance, skill, or presence but because the two people are seen as one entity.

Our experience in the professional world was, for me, a mirror of what was happening in our joint work. In a "good" way, I had lost the ability to identify which ideas or sentences were attached to Smith and which to me. This common experience for collaborators testifies to the deep connection around the work. These ideas and sentences did not "belong" to either one of us, they were created out of the relationship and could not have come from either of us alone. But it was also true that the collaboration was taking on an identity of its own, we were becoming one. We could finish each other's sentences. We could substitute for each other in the classroom. The content of our lectures was becoming more and more similar. The overlap of the Berg and Smith professional circles was growing and the areas unique to each of us that fell outside that overlap *felt* at risk of disappearing.

Rosso and Lukins had a similar experience. The preface to their last joint cookbook included reflections on their relationship that touch on many of the themes in this chapter. They reflect on what it felt like to create together. They report on the ways in which they became "one" in language, clothing, and in the eyes of the world around them. Finally, they reflect on the differences that made the relationship so lively and so successful and that now have brought them to a point where they want to return to their *individual* kitchens to "rethink and restock."

> We have a creative relationship that just seems to keep getting better and better with age. Ideas for recipes sometimes come from an ingredient, a texture, a need to update a classic or a dish we've tasted. We talk it over and improve the concept, cook it, taste it, and critique it together ... then we make adjustments and taste it again.
>
> We've become great friends over these past twelve years. We respect each other, finish each other's sentences, have ideas simultaneously, and have been known to show up in almost the same outfits. We just clicked long ago, and we're blessed with similar timetables, expectations, curiosities, and standards of taste.
>
> But we are two different people, even though we are often confused one for the other. Sheila ... Richard ... and their teenage daughters ... live in Manhattan. Julee recently married to Bill, divides her time between Manhattan and a cottage on Lake Michigan.
>
> Eventually, however, we determined that it was time to shift gears. For too long our schedules had kept us away from the people we wanted to share meals with – not just on weekends or at a special work-night dinner, but all the time. We began to take a long, hard look at our own kitchens, rethinking and restocking them in keeping with all that we had learned over the years.[3]

It is paradoxical that as two become one, as two people create a unique piece of work by combining their differences, this fusion of talent and perspective sets in motion forces to drive them apart. These forces, ironically, derive their power from the same source that animated the collaboration in the first place: The differences between the two collaborators. The loss of those differences, the evolution of one collaborative mind, begins a process of necessary separation. The collaborators need to reclaim their individuality, and their critical differences, for the collaboration to continue. Working together now requires them to work apart. They must return to the roots that nourished their differences. At a minimum, they must leave the bubble that has become the collaborative environment to recharge the batteries that made the collaboration spark. The longer a collaboration lasts, the more the collaborators need time away from it to sustain it. Collaborators can *work* together for decades without separating, but it is very difficult for them to *create* together if they have not spent time outside the collaborative relationship.

In *Tomorrow and Tomorrow and Tomorrow* Sadie, after years of collaboration with Sam, during which, not incidentally, Sadie experiences credit being given to Sam for their joint work, Sadie feels the need for time apart.

> We're barely speaking, and things haven't been good for us for some time. I don't see how we can work together … I don't think we're breaking up forever. But I do think the two of us need some time apart so that we can like each other again. And maybe it is more me than him. But I *want* to do something on my own. Something that is fully mine. Something that no one can attribute, for better or worse, to Sam.[4]

Zevin, the author and a gamer herself, puts into Sadie's mouth both the pain and the necessity of getting out from under a relationship that has erased her individual identity.

As in the case of tension caused by a frayed connection, the tension caused by a collaboration that erodes the individual differences of its partners can become the source of conflict ("things haven't been good for us for some time"), withdrawal ("We're barely speaking") or both. The fundamental purpose of this conflict and withdrawal is to propel some necessary separation ("I want to do something on my own."). Successful collaborations can bind people to each other in ways that stifle their individual development. The world outside the collaboration may look to the pair for their next product – operetta, technology innovation, scientific discovery, marketing plan – often with the expectation that this next product will be like the previous ones in terms of sales, impact, or insight. This expectation, a function of the success of the collaboration, can feel constraining to the people involved. They came together to create, not to replicate. In some cases, collaborations continue to create in the face of pressure to produce or even because of pressure to produce. But in other cases, the pressure to replicate their success causes one or both collaborators to flee the relationship in order to free their creative energy.

Recognizing the Signals

The signs that a collaboration is being driven apart by the fraying of the connection or the erasure of individuality are not subtle. Conflict in one form or another is central to this process since it is often the easiest way to generate the separation needed by the relationship. The way the conflict shows up in the relationship can seem to point the collaborators not to a *relationship* challenge but to an *individual* problem. A romantic partner who works a lot could be a workaholic or they could be avoiding something in the relationship with their significant other. Von Hofmannsthal expressed his frustration with Strauss's lack of timely responses to his correspondence (albeit gently) as if this lack of response was a character flaw in Strauss rather than an indication of a latent conflict in their relationship.[5] If a conflict is understood by the collaborators as an individual problem the result may still be separation, but the misdiagnosis, the lack of attention to the relationship, makes it much more difficult for the collaboration to address the underlying issues. This is not uncommon in close relationships, both personal and professional. Relationship difficulties, like the ones we have outlined in collaborations, are often experienced and approached as if the problem is rooted in one or the other individual, thereby obscuring the relational source. I reproach my wife because she is leaving crumbs on the counter, and I feel put upon to clean them up. She responds by complaining about the "fact" that I leave dishes in the sink that she needs to wash. Off we go, poking at the individual indications of a relational strain around responsibilities and equity.

Another source of being driven apart is the feeling by one or both collaborators that they are not being appropriately recognized, credited, or compensated for their contributions to the shared work. The essence of collaboration is the fact that the parties involved believe that neither of them alone could have created what they produced together. This is not a statement about effort or labor, but rather a shared attestation to the creativity that is born of their relationship. This means that the contributions of the two collaborators are both *necessary* for the creative work. These contributions may not be equal nor equivalent, but both are required. In a real sense, and certainly in the emotional experience of almost all collaborators, their success is a joint success. Take either of the collaborative pieces away and the work each person undertakes alone is not and cannot be the same as the work they produced together. Doudna on her relationship with Charpentier, "The collaboration was fantastic. The intensity of it, the shared ideas. Our differences were a good thing. Not sure either of us would have done it without the other."[6]

When tension over credit, acknowledgment, or recognition arises in a collaboration it is often rooted in the feeling that this fundamental "truth" about collaboration has been ignored. In some cases, one collaborator feels that it has been ignored by the other. One has spoken about the collaboration in a way that diminishes the importance of the other. Or, in navigating their differences, one of the collaborators has been dismissive of an idea or proposal from the other. In other cases, one of the collaborators may feel that people outside the collaboration are ignoring the fundamental truth by attributing the work to only the other collaborator. This lack of recognition or credit can take many forms. Something as seemingly trivial as the order in which the collaborators' names are mentioned or published can set off a conflict between collaborators. Bud

Costello, upset that he was always second in the billing of the highly successful comedy duo "Abbot and Costello" once proposed that the name of the act be changed to "Costello and Abbot."[7] The frequency with which one or the other collaborator is invited to speak about their joint work or the public recognition of only one of the collaborators can spark envy and jealousy. And, of course, if there are financial benefits that are unequally distributed, this too can be experienced as a violation of the fundamental truth of a collaboration.

In all these cases, the tension and conflict over credit and recognition is the concrete representation of a relationship in which one or both collaborators feel unseen. This feeling of not being seen (either by the other collaborator or by a wider community) is an indication of either a frayed relationship or a fused identity. In the former instance, the fraying of the relationship may point to the struggle to manage their differences.For example, have the two collaborators talked about their relative contributions and the implications for how they divide up the financial and professional benefits that follow from their joint work? If the world outside the collaboration places more value on the background, identity, or pedigree of one of the collaborators, can the relationship find a way to incorporate this "reality" without succumbing to it? In the latter case, the fear of a fused identity is the fear that one's individuality will be erased by the brightness of the collaboration. Two names are always said in the same breath, sometimes confused for each other. Lou Costello hated being called Bud Abbot, a not-infrequent occurrence.[8] Here again the challenge for the relationship is to manage the very real possibility that a successful collaboration can make it difficult to see the individuals involved, difficult for both the outside world and the two people themselves.

This last point may require some explanation. It may be obvious that a successful collaboration fuses the two collaborators in the eyes of the public. Watson and Crick, for example, "discovered" the DNA double helix. Outside of the scientific community, most people would have trouble describing Watson or Crick and would be unable to distinguish between them. How many times has someone asked, "Which one is Laurel, and which one is Hardy?" Laurel and Hardy are a comedy team, like Abbot and Costello (which one is Abbot?). Less obvious is the situation in which the collaborators themselves begin to lose awareness of their own contributions to the work. The fact that I cannot remember who wrote which sentences or who had which ideas in my work with Smith, underscores the joint nature of our work. This loss of self is an indication of the power of the collaboration. But this loss of self can lead to a desire to be seen as an individual, a desire for recognition or acknowledgment made stronger by an uncertainty about my own contribution.

Betrayal

Betrayal is a strong word for what collaborators can experience in the course of their work together, but it is sometimes accurate. Betrayal only occurs in intimate relationships, relationships in which the parties have come to trust each other. More specifically, a trusting relationship is one in which we have shared our vulnerabilities and come to believe that the other will not exploit or disregard them in the service of their own needs or desires. When these vulnerabilities are disregarded, the reaction is hurt and rage. The intensity of the emotions released stems from the depth of the trust. The more trusting the relationship, the more intense the sense of betrayal. The collaborative process requires a great deal of trust. If one person is feeling the need to separate, the decision to enact that feeling can be experienced as both a judgment and a betrayal.

It is not unusual for people in a collaboration to also work with others. This feels like a betrayal when the relationship is being driven apart for any of the reasons we have identified. An outside (of the collaboration) working relationship that was acceptable to both people can evolve into one that feels like a betrayal. The act of creating something with someone else can feel to the one left behind as a betrayal of a commitment to be faithful to the primary creative relationship. It can also be experienced as an attempt to sabotage or undo the collaboration. In some cases that is precisely the purpose, especially when one person feels swallowed by the collaboration with no way out, no way to reassert or rediscover themselves. The betrayal rips the trust in the relationship and, at a minimum, pushes the two people apart.

By all accounts, the relationship between Bundini Brown and Mohammed Ali was very close. Brown's son had a close relationship with Ali. The two men were like brothers. But there were times of estrangement as well. As George Foreman, a heavyweight champion himself recalled, "Bundini was in big trouble because I fought Joe Frazier and there Drew Bundini was, screaming and cheering, proud of me. Ali found out about it and suspended him because of that."[9] The so-called "Foreman betrayal" caused serious discord in the relationship between Ali and Brown, but the tensions had been brewing. Why else would Brown be in Foreman's corner for a big fight in the first place?

As we have seen, Hugo Von Hofmannsthal, junior to the world-renowned Richard Strauss, was sensitive about his relationship with the more senior composer. He is appreciative when Strauss accepts his changes or criticisms. He is accepting but not pleased with Strauss's untimely replies to his letters. Strauss on his part appears mildly annoyed at Von Hofmannsthal's emotional reactions to disagreements. All of this is in the context of a creative and successful collaboration. It is striking to read Von Hofmannsthal's reaction to a critical review written by "a member of your (Strauss's) circle." The tone of his letter conveys pent-up frustration with his lack of credit for their joint work. Von Hofmannsthal's vitriol toward the music critic and composer Gustav Brecher belies a deep feeling of betrayal by Strauss. How dare Strauss consort with this person he seems to be saying, though consort Strauss obviously did.

> I should have liked to see you before I leave and would have preferred to say rather than to write what follows. Kessler handed me, as from you, a letter from G. Brecher which has somewhat annoyed me, and it did so because Brecher is a member, even if a subordinate one of your circle. Coming from a writer who is fairly close to you, I consider this letter lacking in respect towards me and therefore objectionable. I can easily overlook the fact that malicious journalists make my share in our joint work from time to time (as it happens again and again) the butt of some resentment that is really meant for you (it was you yourself, I think, who used the very telling expression "lightening conductor"). I should, on the other hand, take a very poor view if, among your circle of protégés, there were to be any lack of understanding or lack of appreciation of the significance, to you, of my collaboration in these three stylistically so very different works … It might *perhaps* have been just as well to publish the text without the comment … but it offers no excuse for such effrontery from subordinate creatures who have never produced anything creative in their lives.[10]

Betrayal is often asymmetrical. One person in the collaboration feels that the relationship is not working before the other or experiences tensions in the relationship that the other has not felt. In hierarchical collaborations, the subordinate's feeling that they are not being recognized or credited can lead them to feel betrayed by the supervisor's investment in other direct reports. The supervisor may have little awareness that their relationships with other subordinates are stirring feelings of betrayal. In fact, these "other" relationships may not spark feelings of betrayal until the tension around recognition becomes an issue. A composer's decision to work with another librettist can be experienced as a statement about the insufficiencies of the librettist's contribution or perhaps more accurately the staleness of a collaboration that has come to rely on a formula rather than the creative tension that once drove their work. When, for whatever reason, the collaborators have not been able to address the current dynamics in the relationship, the librettists can feel betrayed by the composer's decision. A break in the relationship, temporary or permanent, may be needed, but it is extremely difficult for both parties to acknowledge this at the same time. One collaborator comes to realize that they need a change before the other. The feelings of betrayal that result make it even more challenging for the two people to confront and address the evolved tensions in their collaboration.

The breakup of the Beatles illustrates what happens when a relationship needs time apart, but one person gets their first. In describing Lennon's relationship with Yoko Ono in 1968, McCartney acknowledged that the band was "headed toward" a breakup.[11] The implication from McCartney is that Ono was a precipitating factor rather than a causal one. Lennon gave his account in an interview.

> I was too scared to break away from the Beatles, but I had been working on it since 1965 when we stopped touring. And maybe Paul had been too. I don't know. But I made a movie...which never got seen much but did me a lot of good. It did me a lot of good to be away, and it was a withdrawal.[12]

The popular imagination has a third party breaking up the group. The two primary collaborators tell a different story, one in which the Beatles were coming to the end of their productive collaboration. Lennon acted on the *shared* need for separation first, and it felt, perhaps a little to McCartney and a lot to Beatles' fans, like a betrayal.

Like the Beatles, most intimate partnerships struggle with how to confront together the evolution of their relationship. One person may have tried to raise an issue with the other only to feel rebuffed ("Can we talk about this later?"). Both people may have avoided confronting their concerns for fear that any conflict might ruin the relationship ("You get so upset when I raise any issue for discussion.") One of the collaborators may feel blindsided by the other's criticisms of the relationship ("I never knew you felt this way."). When one or both in the relationship are unable or unwilling to examine the inevitable strains that emerge in any collaboration, the chances of betrayal, both real and experienced, go up. The betrayal (or the perception of a betrayal by the other) communicates in ways that neither person has been able to convey verbally, that something is broken in the relationship.

Collaborations are often described and experienced as being driven apart by the in involvement of a third party as in the example of Yoko Ono and the Beatles. This third person, a love partner, close friend, or family member of one of the collaborators, "advises" one of them on the potential benefits of going solo. The motive for giving this advice varies. Some advisors see personal gain, for themselves or for the collaborator (money, fame, exposure, validation) growing out of a split in the collaboration. Others feel that the person they admire, and support is being used or underappreciated in the relationship. In all cases, the message is that the time has come to leave the collaboration and that the advantages of doing so are substantial.

The real question is, what makes a collaborator susceptible to the message in these whispered words? Othello *listens* to Iago when the latter tells him about Desdemona's betrayal. Provided "proof" of her infidelity, Othello doesn't ask his beloved about it, he jumps to the conclusion of betrayal and murderously ends the relationship. Wouldn't you give a loved partner the opportunity to provide her side of the story? Not if you were already primed to believe the whispered words. Not unless you already believed the relationship was doomed.

Many times, the message delivered by the third party has actually come from the collaborator. The friend or family member has been listening to the "complaints" that have emerged as the collaboration has evolved. The complainer may not even be aware that they are complaining or the extent to which their complaints pepper their conversations with this trusted other. But eventually, the friend replays these complaints in the form of advice, advice that has its roots in the collaborator's experience. In these cases, the collaborator's susceptibility to the message stems from the role the friend is playing: "I'm just telling you what I hear when you talk about this relationship."

A third party may see the signs of a fraying relationship before one of the collaborators, or a lover may sense the loss of identity before their partner. If, one day or over time, the advice to consider separating begins to make sense, it is because the collaborator has begun to feel these tensions too. No matter what the motivation for the whispered words, self-serving or genuinely concerned, the willingness to listen to them reveals the forces that have already begun to fuel the desire for some separation. It is rare that a third party *drives* a separation, though this is a popular narrative. The triangulation of another person into the collaboration, someone to talk to about frustrations or concerns, is a destabilizing event for any pair. Often, this is the point of involving the third party. They are enlisted by one of the collaborators in the service of the desire for some separation, as a catalyst for moving apart.

Colin, an academic, and Jerry, a public sector manager (names have been changed), were collaborating on a book about urban policy. The collaboration was a creative connection across professional fields, but it foundered, in part on the issue of appropriate "credit." The apparent voice of this concern was Colin's wife, who Colin reported was telling him that he "deserved" more credit for the book since he was doing most of the writing and it was, after all, an academic book. As we discussed Colin's *wife's* reactions, it became clear to the three of us that the feelings were Colin's, expressed to his wife and then through her back into the collaborative relationship.[13]

Another indicator of tensions driving a collaboration apart, especially tensions involving the loss of individual identity is the sense by a collaborator that they are capitulating or submitting to the proposals, ideas, or strong feelings of the other. When facing the inevitable tensions that arise during collaboration it is tempting to reduce those tensions by simply giving in. The emotional strain on the individuals and on the relationship can lead either one to submit to the other. In the moment that submission seems to reduce the tension. The intensity level might be reduced. Raised voices may be lowered. The stalemate, born of differing perspectives, might be eased yielding a way forward. In the long run, however, surrender leads to separation. The promise of a collaboration is about meaningful and necessary mutual contribution. Giving in to a collaborator, especially repeatedly and without an explicit examination of the reasons for the capitulation, represents a violation of that promise. The "winner" is accepting a shift to dominance rather than mutuality and the "loser" is accepting the loss of their individual identity. Eventually, one or both collaborators will realize that they are no longer in a functioning collaboration and seek a separation.

Unlike a separation that follows a conflict stemming from the differences each brings to the relationship, this separation stems from the absence of difference. One of the collaborators has decided to allow the collaboration to become the work of one individual. Perhaps the emotional toll of creative tension is not worth the potential output. Perhaps the capitulation is the final response to not being accepted or engaged. Perhaps it's just less hassle to give in. The loss of one person's voice in a two-person process puts an end to the collaboration. It's as if, during a musical duet, one of the singers began to sing softly, then only mouthed the words and finally stopped singing altogether.

The presence of conflict, of course, is not simply or usually a sign of a collaboration in trouble. Conflict comes with the work of collaboration. But it is also the manifestation of the essential threat buried in all collaborations, the possibility that the differences are too great and cannot productively coexist, the possibility that a mutual commitment to a good idea or to a longstanding relationship will not be enough to overcome the differences that emerge. If we cannot engage our differences, and this will entail some conflict, raw or refined, then we have no collaboration. If we do engage these same differences, then we risk falling apart or running from each other to escape the metaphorical flames.

When trying to assess whether a conflict indicates a relationship in need of some help, either through time spent apart or time examining the tension, the magnitude of the conflict does not necessarily give us the answer. Big blow-ups can be productive, cathartic, instructive, or reparative. They can finally bring an issue out in the open that has been simmering for a long time. The issue may be about the product or about the relationship. The conflict can be a necessary step in keeping the work or the relationship healthy, able to contain the expression of and engagement with differences. Similarly, small, seemingly trivial conflicts can point to something deeper, especially if these "minor" annoyances keep emerging in one or the other collaborator. In my experience, the little conflicts are more likely to indicate a larger issue because, paradoxically, the larger the underlying issue, the greater the threat to the collaboration and the less likely either collaborator wants to touch it. A minor annoyance presents no threat to the relationship and is therefore easier to express. But because it is "minor" there is a good chance the annoyance is dismissed without any inquiry into the possibility that this trivial conflict, this rattle in the engine of the collaboration, is more than just a loose screw. It was reported that Bud Abbot and Lou Costello separated for a time and Costello would not appear together with Abbot on screen because Abbot had hired a "domestic servant" who Costello had recently fired.[14] Treating "trivial" conflicts seriously can reveal more significant tensions, tensions that can drive a collaboration apart.

Endnotes

1 David Eden, *Gilbert and Sullivan: The Creative Conflict* (Rutherford: Fairleigh Dickinson University Press, 1986).
2 Personal interview.
3 Julee Rosso and Sheila Lukins, *The New Basics Cookbook* (New York: Workman Publishing Company, 1996).
4 Gabrielle Zevin, *Tomorrow, and Tomorrow, and Tomorrow* (New York: Knopf, 2022).
5 Franz H. Bartsch (Ed), *Letters of Hugo von Hofmannsthal and Richard Strauss* (Princeton: Princeton University Press, 1991).
6 Personal interview.
7 Bob Thomas, *Bud and Lou: The Abbott and Costello Story* (New York: Putnam, 1977).
8 'Inside Lou Costello and Bud Abbott's Decades-Long Friendship,' *Closer Weekly* (July 15, 2022), https://www.closerweekly.com/posts/inside-lou-costello-and-bud-abbotts-decades-long-friendship/.
9 Todd Snyder, *Bundini: Don't Believe the Hype* (Boston, MA: Hamilcar Publications, 2020).
10 Franz H. Bartsch (Ed.), *Letters of Hugo von Hofmannsthal and Richard Strauss* (Princeton: Princeton University Press, 1991).
11 Paul McCartney and Paul Muldoon, *A Life in Lyrics*, Podcast (New York: Pushkin Industries, October 18, 2023).
12 David Sheff and G. Barry Golson, *The Playboy Interviews with John Lennon and Yoko Ono* (New York: Berkley Books, 1981).
13 Personal interviews.
14 Bob Thomas, *Bud and Lou: The Abbott and Costello Story* (New York: Putnam, 1977).

Chapter 8

Pulled Apart

In the previous chapter, we explored the ways in which both difference and the evolving lack of differentiation can drive a collaborative relationship apart. In both cases, the tension can make itself felt in concrete, recognizable ways. These concrete indications can be viewed as invitations to step back from the relationship, enabling both people to examine the impact of their joint work on their individual work lives. As we have discussed, these tensions are normal parts of managing a creative process across personal and professional differences. They are often painful and disruptive. They can lead to temporary or permanent pauses in the collaboration. But this too is characteristic of collaborations.

The external forces that *pull* collaborations apart are also normal in these creative pairings. They occur frequently, can be anticipated, and are stimulated by the collaborative relationship itself. And like the internal forces that *push* people apart, these external, pulling forces can occasion a necessary period of separation. The tensions these forces create can also be painful and disruptive. The major difference, however, is that the forces that pull collaborations apart can rarely be understood as invitations to a deeper examination of the relationship.

The power behind these pulling apart forces derives from the cultures (professional and societal) in which collaborations are embedded. These cultures carry normative beliefs about creativity, difference, and relationships that influence how collaborators experience each other. More importantly, they influence how the wider world sees the collaborative relationship. And this, in turn, translates into how the collaboration is described, characterized, written about, and recognized. These descriptions and characterizations often involve separating or trying to separate the individual contributions of each collaborator. It is not simply the wider culture that seeks to identify the individual contributions of each collaborator, it is also the collaborators themselves, raised in these cultures, who may seek this identification even as they work in tandem.

DOI: 10.4324/9781032701998-8

Cultural commentary about the collaboration, whether stories in a publication, words at a ceremony, awards at a dinner, or gossip by the water cooler, has an impact on the collaborative relationship. When the culture assigns credit and seeks to determine who *actually* did what, it can pry apart the relationship. If the relationship is already susceptible to being pried apart, this separation is even more likely. And for the reasons we outlined in the previous chapter, collaborations are always susceptible to coming apart because of the challenges inherent in connecting across differences.

Two Prize-Winning Examples

We begin with two examples of the power of external, cultural forces to pull on the collaborative bonds. The examples describe a phenomenon that stalks most collaborative relationships. They involve two pairs of Nobel Prize-winning scientists. Much has been written about these relationships, including accounts in their own words. These two relationships are quite different from each other. One is a pair of men, Daniel Kahneman and Amos Tversky, two psychologists, who were awarded the Nobel Memorial Prize in Economics in 2002 for their work on the types of cognitive biases that came to define the field of behavioral economics. The other pair, Jennifer Doudna and Emmanuelle Charpentier are two women awarded the Nobel Prize in Chemistry in 2020. They pioneered the development of the CRISPR process for editing genes, the first all-female team to win a Nobel Prize. Both collaborations are illustrative of the themes we have outlined in this book. The differences in background and style fueled the creativity of the pair and caused some tension along the way. Most important for the topic of this chapter, all four individuals felt strongly that they could not have produced their breakthrough discoveries without the other.

When I embarked on the "empirical" part of this book (identifying and seeking to interview people involved in collaborations) I immediately encountered an example of the outside forces that work to pull these collaborations apart. I asked a basic scientist who I know well how I might contact Doudna or Charpentier. He immediately replied, "There's one really good scientist and one who's not very good at all." I was taken aback by the comment. I knew how the two women had described their collaboration. Each credited the other with the complementary skills and approaches that enabled them, together, to be the first to publish the CRISPR technology. Their words seemed sincere and fit with my evolving definition of collaboration. Here is Jennifer:

> We came from such different backgrounds. We were opposites in many ways. She was petite and stylish. Scientifically we came from different perspectives which meant we had complementary skills. And she was

intrigued by the scientific question. The collaboration was fantastic. Not sure either of us would have done it without the other.[1,2]

But was I being naïve? Were these public statements merely a polite and gracious front? Or was my friend participating in a cultural game of figuring out which *individual* in a collaborative relationship is really driving the creative process?

If you are wondering which of the two women was regarded by my friend as the "good" scientist, you are part of the game. The view that individuals, not relationships, produce creative outcomes is widespread. It begins, in the United States, in our early years in school when we memorize (individual) names and dates. Who wrote the Declaration of Independence? Thomas Jefferson. Except, as with most creative efforts, the story is more complicated. The Continental Congress appointed a *committee* to draft the declaration, and the committee asked Jefferson to create a first draft. He did so with the Virginia Declaration of Rights as his guide, a document written primarily by George Mason. So, who wrote the Declaration of Independence? Might it depend on your understanding of collaboration? Could Jefferson have written the document without the work of George Mason? Would his talent at writing (John Adams, a member of the committee was quoted as saying that the task went to Jefferson because of "the elegance of his pen") have been enough to create the Declaration of Independence?

The search for the dominant individual in a collaboration not only does violence to the collaborative process, but it also does violence to the collaborative relationship. Awards and prizes, whispers at professional meetings, organizational policies and practices that require one person's name or one person's name on the top line all can have an impact on how two people, even two people who cherish each other's contributions, feel about each other. Like the dripping of water on a stone, persistent attempts to disentangle a collaborative creation can ultimately wear away at the relationship. Drip by drip the connection is eroded, and the relationship comes apart.

Kahneman and Tversky, like Doudna and Charpentier, exhibited both the personal and professional differences that were the foundations of their collaborative creativity. By all accounts, Tversky was a charismatic, loud, room-filling type of personality, and Kahneman was his opposite, quiet, soft-spoken, and intense. Both felt and expressed the conviction that their work was the product of a truly collaborative relationship. This feeling was most powerfully expressed by Tversky upon being awarded the MacArthur "Genius Award," an award that in its citation for *Tversky's* worthiness cited only work that had been done collaboratively with Kahneman. Michael Lewis quotes a friend of Tversky's who saw and heard Tversky's reaction to receiving the grant. "He was pissed. He said, 'What are these people thinking? How can they give a prize to just one of the winning pair? Do they not realize they are dealing the collaboration a death blow?'"[3]

The MacArthur Award is a shiny example of a cultural attempt to identify the individual contributions to a collaboration and then to reward one, the perceived primary driver, of the collaborative pair. Tversky's reaction to the award underscores two empirical realities, at least as he saw the world of intellectual discovery. First, the awarding of prizes to an individual who has created something in a relationship with someone else is a distortion of that creative process. The award alters the truth about that process and perpetuates that alteration. An individual honor pulls apart the creative bond and then erases one-half of the collaboration. Second, Tversky makes clear that an award to one collaborator has the potential to destroy the collaborative relationship. He knows, from personal experience, that elevating one-half of a two-person collaboration begins a process of increasing alienation between the collaborators.

In a way that is eerily similar to my story about being introduced with my collaborator's professional biography, Lewis recounts Tversky's efforts to convince editors, awards committees, professional associations, and even students that the work that was now making him famous was a joint product. One author used Tversky's name to identify one of his and Kahneman's discoveries, calling it the "Tversky effect." Tversky first pointed out that the "effect" in question had been developed by the two men in collaboration. He went on to say that if only one name should be attached to this phenomenon, it should be Kahneman since he was the first to observe it in the real world.[4] These comments to whoever would listen had no impact on the way the United States treated Tversky. He, and most often he alone, was cited in publications, invited to give talks, consult with governments, and receive awards. And the persistent distortion of the collaboration, reducing it to the work of one person, had a significant impact on the relationship between Tversky and Kahneman.

From a highly creative, intellectually sparkling collaboration, the relationship between Tversky and Kahneman began to unravel. Kahneman was the force behind the separation. It was his preference to stop their joint work. It no longer felt joint. Lewis explains it this way,

> It had taken Danny the longest time to understand his own value. Now he could see that the work Amos had done alone was not as good as the work they had done together. The joint work always attracted more interest and higher praise than anything Amos had done alone. It had apparently attracted the Genius Award. And yet the public perception of their relationship was now a Venn diagram, two circles, with Danny wholly contained by Amos. The rapid expansion of Amos's circle pushed his borders further and further away from Danny's.[5]

Kahneman's words express the essence of collaborative creativity, the experience of producing something "better" than either could have produced alone. It also expresses the pain of getting lost in the shadow of your collaborator's reputation and notoriety. Finally, and most relevant to this chapter, Kahneman lays the responsibility for this gradual dissolution of the relationship on "public perception." Undoubtedly, the personal differences in style, "charisma," and approach also figured into the way in which the public reacted to the two men. But both Tversky and Kahneman felt strongly that the external world's relentless attention to an *individual* rather than to a *relationship* had contributed to pulling them apart.

Before we leave Nobel Prize winners, let's return to Jennifer Doudna and Emmanuelle Charpentier. In the months following the Nobel award, these two world-class scientists received several subsequent prizes, many of them jointly and some together with other scientists who had participated in the competitive research process that had culminated in the discovery of the CRISPR gene editing technique. In their case, the strain engendered by the outside world was driven primarily by the commercial implications of this technology. Many parties, including both Doudna and Charpentier, attempted to wade into the world of commercial application with an inclusive approach, an approach that sought to bring together the dozens of scientists who had been working on the numerous aspects of the CRISPR technology. These efforts all broke down in the face of institutional, financial, and personal interests.[6]

The world of high-level scientific research has, for the last century at least, been a powerful mixture of collaboration and competition. In many ways, collaboration both within a lab and between labs, is the essence of scientific advancement. It allows progress to happen across areas of specialization and it enables simultaneous investigations on pieces of the same puzzle. It is also extremely competitive – for funding, fame, and future opportunities. As the pressure from outside interests converged on the scientists, including Doudna and Charpentier, many of the scientific relationships involved in CRISPR research became strained. Patent applications, for example, the foundation of any commercial venture, require that the original source of a piece of intellectual property be identified. The first person (or team, but usually a *person*) to identify a protein or a process had a better chance of being granted a patent. As a result, lawyers and institutional stakeholders began to parse collective work into individual accomplishments. For Doudna and Charpentier, what had once been a stimulating and productive collaboration in the truest sense of the term fell prey to the search for an individual pioneer. Walter Isaacson's book on the discovery of the CRISPR technology is titled *The Code Breaker* and Jennifer Doudna's picture is on the cover.[7] The title is not "Code Breakers" or even "The Code Breakers." The title he chose and the picture that went with it suggest an individual accomplishment even as the story Isaacson tells involves an entire cast of scientists. A single leading figure was offered up to capture the imagination (and perhaps the financial backing) of the American public.

Doudna and Charpentier drifted apart in the years following the Nobel award. Their separation, as Doudna described it,[8] was a source of sadness. It seemed to be the result of "patent fights, prizes, companies," external sequelae to the scientific collaboration, a relationship that Doudna characterized as "fantastic, intense and full of shared ideas." Realities external to their relationship shaped their ultimate professional and personal estrangement. Both women participated in these unfolding events, but both, each in their own way, tried to change the trajectory they knew would be imposed on them by the outside world. Perhaps their experience of collaboration in the world of science, both with each other and with many other collaborators, led each of them to propose collaboration outside of science, with venture capitalists, lawyers, and research institutions. To the extent that those efforts failed, and they often did, the failure left in place a world that slowly but inexorably pulled them apart.

Rosso and Lukins

Remember the collaborative team of Rosso and Lukins that created *The Silver Palate Cookbook*? A handful of years after the publication of their final cookbook, the relationship between Rosso and Lukins was over. The break appeared to be sudden and tied to a paragraph about Lukins that Rosso included in a newsletter sent to her food community that, in Lukins's eyes, violated Lukins's personal privacy for Rosso's public gain.[9] A solid relationship might have weathered such a wound. The fact that the two partners reportedly never spoke after this event suggests that the fracture lines were already in place. Their decision a few years earlier to return to their individual kitchens further suggests that they were both feeling a desire or need for separation.[9]

The aftermath of the triggering event seems to indicate that the world around these two women had been pulling apart their respective contributions to the collaboration for some time. "It was well known," said a caterer who worked with Rosso and Lukins, "that Julee was wonderful with ideas ... she was the ideas person. But she did not cook."[10] In the world of cookbooks, it is not hard to imagine that when you pull apart a collaboration it is the "cook" who gets the lion's share of the (individual) credit. It is much harder for the group of cooking professionals to believe that one of their own might not have been as successful without the contributions of the "non-cook," the marketing and promotion expert, and the "ideas" person who proposed the business in the first place. In this case, the outside world may not have been the only force separating these collaborators, their own words tell us that they were both ready for some time apart, but as with other collaborations, the world around this one had been parsing this relationship, trying to determine which of the two had been the driving force behind its success. The newsletter "exploitation" may have been an affront that catalyzed the sharp and permanent separation that followed.

Why Pull It Apart?

The experience of collaboration almost always involves two people coping with or managing the reactions of the world around them to their joint work. Sometimes these reactions are benign, at least on the surface. Names are confused. Credit is mistakenly or unevenly assigned. Sometimes the reactions are expressions of misattributions rooted in the history of gender and race relations or assumptions about age, expertise, and seniority. Von Hofmannsthal expressed his belief that the reason he was overlooked by journalists was because of Strauss's fame and reputation.[11] Gabrielle Zevin, the author of *Tomorrow and Tomorrow and Tomorrow*, said in an interview,

> I have a male partner and we've made films together, and I have had the experience of being called his wife in a major newspaper. I am not his wife. We are not married. It is just a way to minimize my contribution.[12]

These reactions, revealing cultural biases, perpetuate, whether intentionally or not, both the misattributions and their consequences for the individuals and groups affected. In many cases, the reactions have come from people and institutions actively seeking to dissect the collaboration, to literally cut it apart to identify the part each individual played in the joint work. Once identified, the final step in the dissection is to assign the "lead" to one or the other of the collaborators. The search for the *individual* basis of a *collaborative* product is common and forms a societal backdrop to collaborative work.

Why does this happen? What is it about collaboration or about the human experience more broadly that might explain this need for dissection? Human beings create, accomplish, and survive in social units, in relationship to each other. Self-sufficiency is the exception rather than the rule in human development. For humans, development appears to have involved both individual-level characteristics that advantage survival directly (hair, skin, bone, gut, brain) as well as individual characteristics that advantage survival through their impact on social or collaborative behavior (empathy, language, brain). We are not the only species that cooperates (and even collaborates) to survive. All the more curious that many collaborative efforts are met with an impulse, both intellectual and emotional, to pull them apart by the world in which they are embedded.

What follows are my attempts to answer this question. These answers will serve as partial guideposts for the subsequent chapters on how to manage the dynamics of collaborative relationships, especially the challenge of being pulled apart. I offer three broad classes of explanation. The first is a cultural explanation that briefly explores the influence of the individualistic nature of the United States (and other Western nations). The emphasis on the individual as the agent of change, accomplishment, and inventiveness throughout history makes it difficult to see and conceptualize the role of collaborative relationships. The second explanation returns to the role our group memberships play in drawing us back from our engagements with members of other groups. As we outlined earlier, these group memberships bring with them skills, perspectives, and training, the raw material of creative connection. But they also bring with them allegiances, loyalties, expectations, and in many cases, an ethnocentric view of other groups. Finally, I explore some of the psychological factors that may contribute to the efforts to deconstruct a collaboration. What is it about the intimate nature of a truly collaborative relationship that is unsettling to others outside the collaboration?

An Individualized Curriculum

In the United States, education about the centrality and importance of the individual begins early and continues throughout life. Individual rights and freedoms are at the core of our history classes. We learn about events and the individuals who drove or authored those events. We memorize famous names. Who was Alexander the Great? Julius Caesar? Who invented the cotton gin? The steam engine? The phonograph and telephone? We learn when these individuals lived and what made them famous. Of course, there are many prejudices revealed in the list of individuals we memorize from elementary school through college and beyond. Each of these names reveals lenses – gendered, racialized, nationalized – through which human history is refracted and taught. One lens is rarely considered, even today when many of the incomplete and skewed understandings of history are beginning to be revised. We rarely look at historical events through the lens of significant and influential relationships.

We do look at the influence of individuals on other individuals. Artists whose work owes much to the influence of other artists. Inventors who built on the work of previous inventors. Philosophers whose ideas stem from the writings of those who came before them or were developed to address the formulations of others in their field. And we occasionally learn about social or political movements. But outside of historical scholarship, our educational system rarely examines how relationships gave rise to inventions, legislation, and discoveries, preferring often to delve into the backgrounds of individual historical actors for explanations of events. Even when two names are associated with accomplishment: Lewis and Clark, Wilbur and Orville Wright, Martin Luther King, Jr., and Ralph Abernathy; most of us learn little about how the *relationship* contributed to that accomplishment. As a result, our education deposits within us an implicit understanding that creative accomplishment is an individual task, a function of individual talent and persistence.

The way we assess teaching and learning, reinforces this didactic message. We measure "success" individually whether by testing or portfolio assessment. We promote students through the educational system based on individual measures of success, measures that purport to assess individual traits, usually mental traits, associated with future educational and vocational accomplishment. Here again these attempts at measuring individual "intelligence," "aptitude," and "talent" also reveal the prejudices of the societies in which they were developed. I contend we also fail to examine another prejudice, an assumption of the primacy of *individual* agency throughout history, an assumption that validates our assessment approach.

A change in perspective is possible, but given the educational emphasis on individual accomplishment, it is difficult. Years ago, a colleague's adult son received a grant to develop a history curriculum that was centered on the actions and accomplishments of groups. His envisioned was a companion curriculum to the "standard" history syllabus that would not only highlight the role of relationships (especially groups of co-actors) but also explore what made these relationships work, and what characteristics of their connections to each other enabled their creativity or effectiveness. As far as I know, the curriculum was never implemented anywhere. Without a framework that points us toward the role of relationships in human accomplishment, we are unlikely to see these relationships even when they are all around us. If our radio only receives one frequency, we can only hear the music on that one channel. We may come to believe that it is the only channel broadcasting. And when other sounds force their way into our earphones, we may not know how to interpret them. We may experience these new sounds as "noise" and attempt to filter out what we do not recognize, leaving us with a signal with which we are familiar.[13]

In my field, organizational psychology, the strongest signal is the individual explanation for organizational events. In a case I teach, seminar participants of all backgrounds and ages, when faced with a description of a troubling organizational scenario, invariably and repeatedly offer individual-level explanations for what is occurring. "John is a jerk." "John is insecure." "The team leader is ineffective." "The team leader has lost control of the meeting." Despite multiple data points in this one-page case that suggest other factors might be involved in explaining the events described (e.g., giggles and laughter in the room, demographic characteristics of the members of the team, elements of the situation), the first six or eight explanations are always individual-level ones.[14,15]

A bias toward individual agency can also be observed in real-life cases. In an era when students were invited to sit in on faculty recruitment and promotion committees (without a vote but with the opportunity to give input and to observe) I was elected by my peers to sit on the promotions committee for the psychology department. My attraction to organizational psychology had been, in part, because of its attention to how human beings worked together. I was interested in how this committee worked and how it assessed the professional accomplishments of the academics above me in the hierarchy. In hindsight, I was terribly naïve about the profession. As the committee began to review the publication lists of the candidates for promotion, it became clear that "joint authored" articles were not counted in the candidates' favor unless it could be determined that the candidate was the driving force behind the ideas in the paper. If the candidate was junior, the presumption was often that the ideas originated in the senior author. If the candidate's name was the second (rather than the first) of two, it was assumed that the first author had been the main contributor. At no time in any of these discussions over many weeks was there ever a discussion about the possibility that a jointly authored article could have been a genuine collaboration, that is, a piece of creative work that neither could have produced alone. I didn't like the message. I didn't agree with its underlying assumption. But I had been educated about the culture of the professional world I was about to enter.

Educational and organizational practices in the United States have worked hard at the process of distinguishing individuals from each other. These practices assess, sort, rank, allocate, train, place, and promote individuals. The quality of these practices varies, but the cultural commitment to them is almost universal. The individual is the primary unit of analysis and investment. As a result, most of us learn to distinguish ourselves from the "pack" to succeed. The combination of institutional practices and personal motivation aimed at individual success can make it difficult for both institutions and individuals to recognize the role of collaboration even when it is happening. We cannot see it, focused as we are on the search for distinguished people and the importance of distinguishing ourselves.

Imagine a team pulled together to tackle a project in a private or public institution. After months of work, they successfully complete the work. Now, the Human Relations (HR) function in the organization, tasked with succession planning, emails the supervisor of this project team, and asks for individual performance reviews of the team members. The supervisor writes back that the team *as a team* was able to succeed because of their collaboration, the project could not have been done by any of the team members alone. The HR representative acknowledges this reality but reiterates their need for the supervisor to identify the "high potential" members of the team. If the supervisor accedes to the HR needs (for obvious reasons) the result echoes Amos Tversky's warning about awards: identifying one part of a collaboration as the driving force distorts the reality of creative collaboration and, more consequentially, it risks destroying the collaborative relationship *and future collaborations* within this organization.

The people in this scenario all feel that they have no choice. All are resigned to their individual and collective fate. What is HR to do with a successful team? There is no "team" personnel file. Another team, even one with some of the same members, might not be as successful. But how do we reward, promote, acknowledge, and invest in a successful *relationship?*[16] Faced with little or no choice we follow our cultural norms. We look to identify the "leader" or "catalyst" on the team. We dissect and separate a creative connection into its parts. We give up on seeing collaboration because we have no institutional place to put what we see, and no promotional path for a successful relationship. We have lots of places to put outstanding individuals, so we look for them.

Several years ago, a conversation with a former colleague illustrated how powerful and ubiquitous the cultural emphasis on the individual is and how much it can obscure the contribution of relationships to human accomplishment. The colleague called me with an idea. He was teaching a course in a business school on the role of groups. The course included a variety of topics on how groups work including decision-making, leadership, motivation, problem-solving, and the like. My colleague considered himself a student of groups and believed in the value of well-functioning groups to organizations. His course created five-person groups at the beginning of the semester. These groups went through exercises together, analyzed cases together, and even examined their own group dynamics together, all in the service of learning about groups. My colleague proposed to me the following idea (which he subsequently implemented). At the end of the semester, he would ask the members of each group to evaluate the contribution of each of the other members of their group on a five-point scale. The student who scored the highest in each group would become a teaching assistant for the class the next semester.

I was shocked at the suggestion. After investing, both experientially and conceptually, in learning about how *groups* contributed to organizational effectiveness, this last assignment asked the students to make *individual* assessments using a single-item criterion. The contributions of the group members, different in kind and impact, were reduced to a score, stripped of both context and connection, and then used to award a plum job in the future. The effect of the assignment, I feared, would be to undermine the premise of the course. If the professor wanted the students to consider how relationships could accomplish or create in ways that individuals alone could not (and one of the exercises in the course was an explicit illustration of just such synergy) what violence to that idea was being done when the professor then enlisted group members in measuring and rewarding one individual from the group? This final activity, in both content and method, tuned the class back to the individual frequency with which they and the business school were most familiar.

Group Allegiances

In previous chapters, I have emphasized group memberships as the source of many of the differences that fuel collaboration. Groups also make demands on their members. Physicians demand allegiance to professional standards and ethical codes for an individual to remain a member of the group in good standing. They may also require participation in regulatory committees as well as financial contributions needed to sustain the group. All groups function similarly. Nation states strive to care for their citizens, providing education, safety net services, and opportunity and in return, they collect taxes and expect that these citizens will not work to actively destroy the group. The survival of any group depends on the involvement and contribution of its members. In simplest terms, if every member of a group ceased to participate in the core activities of the group (educational, professional, commercial, cultural) the group would cease to exist. As a result, collaboration across groups (and most collaborations are across groups) can be experienced by group members as something to be avoided since it siphons time and energy away from the groups to which an individual belongs. Attempts at collaboration may even be punished for the same reason.

When someone invests in a relationship with a member of another group, the implicit (and sometimes explicit) message is that this other group has something to offer. This could easily be viewed as an advantage for the members of a group since collaborations with others who complement what my group has developed can enhance the accomplishments of both groups. What each person in a collaboration learns can be brought back to their "home" group thereby enriching the entire group. But such relationships can also be viewed as a threat. If another group has something to offer, might a collaborator ultimately leave their own group and join the other? The recruitment of the term "collaborator" to describe someone who betrays their own group by joining an "enemy" is relatively recent. In the early nineteenth century, the French word *collaborateur* described someone whose activities aided the monarchy during the Napoleonic wars. The modern meaning of the term comes from the Second World War when it was used to describe traitorous French citizens who cooperated with the Nazis. In addition to the obvious reasons for choosing this word to describe a wartime betrayal, its appeal might also be traced to the fact that any collaboration involves some preference or appreciation for another group over one's own.

Since leaving (intellectually, physically, emotionally) a group is an existential threat to that group, most groups educate their members about the virtues of their own group and the weaknesses of other groups. Many ethnic and religious subgroups in the United States, for example, have special schools for their children to attend (in addition to the public schools) where the children learn about their heritage (e.g., Hebrew Schools, Chinese Schools, Catechism Classes). These schools may or may not be explicit in their instruction about the limitations of other groups, but it could be seen as implicit in the existence of the school itself. Ethnocentrism is a persistent feature of intergroup relations. It serves to bind group members to their (superior) group and thereby ensure the group's survival. Collaboration suggests a chink in the ethnocentric armor created by groups. To value someone from another group means acknowledging their worth and the possibility of our limitations. Valuing the other is often met with a reinforcement of ethnocentric attitudes. The shoring up of our value often takes the form of minimizing or demeaning the value of the other.

For example, when Sullivan began to work with Gilbert on light opera, he was told by other composers that his collaboration was beneath any serious composer and that his craft would suffer because of this joint work.[17] Karen, a basic scientist at a major medical school proposed doing research with a physician in an area of intersecting interests and was told by the chair of her department not to do it. Working with a doctor would not be well regarded by the core members of her field and therefore not worth her time. Jean-Paul Rampal was chided for his foray out of classical music into a collaboration with jazz composer Claude Bolling. The collaboration, he was warned, would diminish his standing as a classical flutist (and perhaps by implication, the standing of all classical flutists).

In Henry James's short story "Collaboration"[18] the novelist provides a compelling account of the anxiety that attends many cross-group collaborations in the way he describes the relationship between Vendemer (a French librettist) and Heidenmauer (a German) composer. Both men are impressed with each other's skills. Heidenmauer exalts at Vendemer's play. "The subject is splendid – it has taken possession of me. Will you do it with me? Will you work with me? Shall we make something great!" But at the thought of this glorious collaboration, Heidenmauer immediately goes to thoughts of his home group, his country. "It will be bad for me in my country. I shall suffer for it. They won't like it. They'll abuse me for it." "They'll hate my libretto so?" asks Vendemer. "Yes, your libretto – they'll say it is immoral and horrible. And they'll say *I'm* immoral and horrible for having worked with you. You'll injure my career. Oh yes, I shall suffer!" "*Et moi donc [and me too]!*" Vendemer exclaims. "I shall also make *you* suffer – I shall nip your prosperity in the bud. In art there are no countries." The animas these two men expect was rooted in a recent war between their two countries. Embedded in a historical moment of pain and conflict between their two groups, the collaboration was imperiled.

Pulling apart a collaboration, especially by demeaning a person or the group they come from underscores the transgression of working across differences, a transgression that risks the solidarity and survival of our home group. If collaboration is allowed, if creativity can arise from the connection across background and training, then the ethnocentric boundary around groups is weakened and the movement of ideas and energy between groups becomes easier, but fears of losing the distinctive nature of group identity can become heightened. When heightened, these fears can lead group members to pull their collaborators back inside the group with threats, enticements, or innuendo. Whether these efforts succeed, they almost always impact the collaborative relationship. None of us is immune from the judgments of the groups to which we belong. When they criticize our collaborator or the collaboration itself, the criticism worms its way into how we see ourselves and our collaborative relationship.

Psychological Reactions to Collaboration

Collaborations can also be dissected and pulled apart for less obvious, but powerful psychological reasons. These reasons are rooted in the intimate nature of the collaborative relationship. As we have discussed, the creative complementarity of a collaboration depends on the sharing of both strengths and weaknesses, a sharing that increases the vulnerability of both people. Like any intimate relationship in which two people are allowed or forced to see the complete other, flaws along with virtues, a collaboration feels "special" and is often seen by others as special. It is different from other relationships. It tends to contain a broader range of intense emotions than most other relationships. Intimate relationships give fuller expression to anger, passion, love, and frustration than casual personal and professional relationships. They share "inside" jokes, silent acknowledgments, and implicit understandings because they know each other in a more complete way. Most collaborative pairs (e.g., Kahneman and Tversky, Rosso and Lukins, Smith and Berg) use the same phrase to describe this intimacy: "We can finish each other's sentences."

The collaborative bubble can arouse mixed feelings in the surrounding world. Along with admiration and appreciation can come unease and discomfort. Private jokes, for example, convey the depth of a relationship but also, by their essence, exclude others. Public displays of affection tend to make people uncomfortable. Why? Perhaps public intimacy stirs deep-seated frustrations with our own (lack of) intimate relations, holding up a mirror to our fears of never developing them. Or the exclusionary nature of intimate relationships may trigger feelings of abandonment or isolation. If we do not see the intimacy, we do not have to contend with these feelings. We can look away, tell the intimate couple to take their intimacy somewhere else or poke holes in the intimate relationship itself to reduce our discomfort.

In the late 1990s a male colleague, 20 years my senior, invited me to write a book with him. We decided to write it as a dialog and constructed our writing as a back-and-forth exchange on a range of topics related to groups. Each chapter title had the author's name underneath the title and often the first sentence referred to our collaborator's previous writing. The style was intimate. We used first names and engaged each other's academic material in an informal way. We might even include personal asides like, "I cannot believe you actually wrote that in your last chapter." We introduced the book with a description of the method and our rationale for the choice: we wanted the reader to see the unfolding of the relationship alongside the unfolding of the ideas. We sent the manuscript to an esteemed academic press, one with which my colleague had previous publishing experience. The reply astounded us both. The editor liked the content but thought the approach was "too intimate" for an academic book. He went on to suggest that readers might "wonder" about the relationship between two men, one senior and one junior. As evidence of the impact of such a reaction on a collaborative relationship, my immediate impulse was to take the book somewhere else. My colleague convinced me to allow him to edit the manuscript to be less intimate in its format so that it would be published.

The editor's comment, coming as it did from a position of power (at least with respect to publishing an academic book!) had a minimal effect on the manuscript but our different reactions to it pulled us away from each other. He moved slightly toward the editor, and I moved away, creating a rift in our relationship. I found myself ceding what should have been joint decisions to my collaborator, going so far once as to suggest that he author the book himself, free to use my contributions without attribution. In this case, the editor's discomfort seemed to us to be rooted in homophobia, but collaborations always connect people across differences and these connections (across race, religion, ethnicity, and social class) have long been a source of intergroup and interpersonal distress. Ours was a small illustration of a group's attempt to forbid a connection with another group in the face of its distress. One need only look at books, plays, and movies to see the artistic expression of this distress (e.g., *Romeo and Juliet, Loving, Fiddler on the Roof, West Side Story, Harold and Maude*) and its consequences.

The other reason those surrounding a collaboration might, however unconsciously, seek to pull it apart is the feelings of jealousy and loss that attend the formation of an intimate relationship. While most of us will admit to feeling happy for a friend or relative who has found an intimate partner, fewer of us will admit to feeling worried about what will happen to *our* relationship with this friend or sister now that they have a special relationship. The fear that we may lose an intimate relationship can cause us to undermine the relationship either directly or indirectly. We may hint to our brother that the "other" is not good enough for him. Or we may gossip to people around us both that the new intimate relationship is flawed or doomed. Even if we do none of this, it is difficult to escape the feeling of loss that comes when someone chooses an intimate relationship with someone else. While it may be true that love and acceptance are not scarce resources, available only to be given to a precious few in our lives, it often feels that way in that moment we observe a close colleague or friend in an intimate relationship with another. When it does, we can become part of the external forces pulling a collaboration apart.

Endnotes

1 Walter Isaacson, *The Code Breaker: Jennifer Doudna, Gene Editing, and the Future of the Human Race* (New York: Simon & Schuster, 2021).
2 Personal interview.
3 Michael Lewis, *The Undoing Project: A Friendship That Changed Our Minds* (New York: W. W. Norton & Company, 2016).
4 Michael Lewis, *The Undoing Project: A Friendship That Changed Our Minds* (New York: W. W. Norton & Company, 2016).
5 Michael Lewis, *The Undoing Project: A Friendship That Changed Our Minds* (New York: W. W. Norton & Company, 2016).
6 Walter Isaacson, *The Code Breaker* (New York: Simon & Schuster, 2021).
7 Walter Isaacson, *The Code Breaker* (New York: Simon & Schuster, 2021).
8 Personal interview.
9 Sheila Lukins and Julee Rosso, *The New Basics Cookbook* (New York: Workman Publishing Company, 1989).
10 Catherine S. Manegold, 'Food Fight,' *Tampa Bay Times*, June 24, 1993.
11 Franz H. Bartsch, *Letters of Hugo von Hofmannsthal and Richard Strauss* (Princeton: Princeton University Press, 1991).
12 Gabrielle Zelin, Interview with Keith Stuart, *The Guardian*, September 20, 2022.
13 Personal communication with Bena Kallick.
14 David Berg, 'Levels of Analysis', published on the Yale Psychiatry Department website (accessed online at https://studylib.net/doc/8393657/levels-of-analysis--diagnosis-and-intervention).

15 Leroy Wells, Jr., 'The Group-as-a-Whole Perspective and its Theoretical Roots,' in Arthur D. Coleman and Marvin H. Geller (Eds.), *Group Relations Reader,* Vol. 2 (Washington DC, 1985), pp. 109–126.
16 Harold Leavitt, 'Suppose we took groups seriously,' in *Readings in Managerial Psychology* (Chicago: University of Chicago Press, 1989), pp. 410–420.
17 Hesketh Pearson, *Gilbert and Sullivan: A Biography* (New York: Harper & Row, 1935).
18 Henry James, 'Collaboration,' in *The Wheel of Time, Collaboration, Owen Wingrave* (New York: Harper & Brothers, 1893), pp. 99–144.

Chapter 9

Staying In

The major conclusions we draw from our inquiry into both the linguistic and experiential nature of collaboration help us think about how to manage these relationships. First, we notice that the different personalities and backgrounds that each collaborator brings are simultaneously a source of stimulation and creativity and a source of tension and conflict. Collaborations do not work well when the differences are minimized or when one of the collaborators "goes silent," that is, stops expressing their unique contribution either because they are consistently not being heard or because not expressing these differing opinions seems to be in the service of preserving harmony in the relationship. Collaborations can also struggle when the characteristics that each person brings to the relationship cannot find a way to co-exist if these different views and skills become conflicting views and skills without a connection strong enough to hold the two people together. It can be tempting to think that individual differences are either the fuel that drives the engine of collaboration or the highly flammable mixture that threatens to blow up this engine. The reality we observe is that the differences at the heart of all collaborations represent both opportunity and peril.

Second, collaborative relationships stir up intense emotions both in the collaborators and often in those around the collaborative pair. Inside the relationship, the intensity and intimacy of a collaboration can evoke envy, competition, and doubt as well as elation, wonder, and appreciation. Collaboration depends on complementarity, on the limitations and strengths of two people meshing to put in motion a process that neither could have initiated alone. As a result, the vulnerability experienced by each collaborator can be intense and unfamiliar. If we are both perfect and complete, we do not need a collaboration. If neither of us is perfect nor complete, we must disclose and discover our respective limitations for the collaboration to take flight. Very few of us are truly comfortable with either disclosing our vulnerabilities or discovering those of others, especially others on whom we depend.

DOI: 10.4324/9781032701998-9

Third, collaborations do not unfold in a vacuum. Each of the collaborators remains connected to the groups and institutions from which they come. The complementary in training, perspective, and experience that propels a collaboration is rooted in these groups and is nourished by each collaborator's continued involvement with them. In addition, these people and organizations often provide crucial financial and emotional support. But these groups and institutions can also pull apart collaborations to maximize the benefit they derive or to perpetuate a cultural investment in the myth of individualism. The awards they bestow and the descriptions they release about collaborative work can weaken collaborative relationships to the point of destroying them. The work of maintaining a collaboration includes addressing the opportunities and threats in the world in which the relationship is embedded.

Finally, collaborative relationships have an ebb and flow. They fluctuate, sometimes wildly, other times gently, between intense connection and necessary separation. The often-unacknowledged reality is that collaborations, like all significant relationships, have ups and downs as the two people learn about each other, evolve as a relationship, and change individually. Our aspirations for a relationship, especially a collaboration, are that the relationship sustains a steady pulse of mutual affection and respect. But of course, this is only an asymptote, a standard that we strive for, coming close at some moments and falling short at other times. Relationships are living, breathing, changing connections. When we are deeply connected, the work and the relationship can be exhilarating. When we are apart, to recharge or reflect, one or both of us can feel "off," estranged from both our collaborator and the joint work. Being connected and being separated are twin elements of the life of collaborative relationships.

Our focus in this chapter is on the challenges of staying connected and staying in the relationship. Five challenges, some originating inside the relationship and others from outside, are each followed by suggestions for managing them in a way that allows the collaborators to stay connected. These five by no means exhaust the challenges faced by collaborations, but they are intended to be representative. The next chapter looks at the challenges collaborations face in letting go or getting out of the relationship. Although this is the less intuitive aspect of collaborations, getting out also needs to be managed by the people involved.

Differences

Differences are challenging. Most people I talk to are supporters of "diversity," the importance of including a variety of backgrounds and perspectives to solve a problem or enrich a discussion. These same people, including me, when faced with a diverse group charged with a task act as if the work would go smoother *if everyone were the same*. This is an understandable wish. In a group of like-minded people with similar backgrounds, an agreement can be easier to reach, proposals easier to outline, and plans easier to implement. At another level, such a wish, if fulfilled, would literally destroy the potential represented by a diverse group. Two-person collaborations can face a similar challenge. They are drawn together by their differences. Their creative output depends on the blending and clashing of those differences. And yet these same differences can be troublesome.

One approach to managing differences, easy to articulate, and much harder to undertake, is to consistently choose to go straight at them. This might mean even exaggerating the differences, if need be, making it possible to confront their implications for the joint work. Differences that cannot be talked about can constrain intimacy because we withhold parts of ourselves out of fear of rejection. The withholding puts distance between two people. Little by little we become strangers rather than intimates. One weekend, long into our relationship, Smith wanted to tell me about a recent experience. It centered around a "spooky" event during which someone who could not have known about a tragic event and its circumstances reported both the event and the circumstances with eerie accuracy. Smith wondered if there were phenomena that affected us but about which we were unaware, an energy that could be transmitted on wavelengths most of us could not receive. I argued, gently at first out of love and respect for my collaborator, that there must be some "rational explanation." I offered a few. At first, he countered my argument with facts ("she did not know the person," "they had no contact," "it was never publicized") and then gave up. I left the conversation upset at myself for not being more accepting, and more open to what Smith was saying and feeling.

A few weeks later, my distress unabated, I called Smith and suggested we talk about that conversation. We talked for a long time. I confessed my distress at my inability to listen and to be accepting and my enduring skepticism about the implications of his thoughts concerning energy, communication, and spooky events. (I used the term "spooky" in the previous paragraph to evoke the quantum physics concept of strange entanglement at a distance.) He told me of his curiosity but also of his confusion and disorientation while living through these events. It was, initially, an uncomfortable conversation. My feelings had their roots in my own self-judgment but also in my fears about what this difference in worldview might do to our relationship. We came away with a deeper understanding of each other. Such an outcome is not guaranteed when such conversations occur. What is almost a guarantee is that avoiding the conversation would have resulted in an expanding pattern of avoidance and, quite possibly, the slow attenuation of our collaboration.

The reason talking through differences needs to be a suggested approach rather than a natural occurrence is because most relationships seek out commonality rather than difference. If similarity brings us into closer contact, differences can cause us to take a step back. Differences, of course, can stimulate and entice, but if they are submerged in the interest of establishing commonality, even the advantages of difference can be unrealized. It is not always easy for us to recognize when we are moving toward similarity and away from difference in our efforts to promote relational comfort. If we do recognize a move away from our differences, it is always best to move toward them. Co-CEOs Sean and Emily found themselves increasingly alienated from each other. The business was in trouble and their differences made it very difficult to work on the problems. Sean, the extrovert, was in favor of experimentation. Things would work out with hard work and commitment. Emily, the introvert, wanted to pursue a more conservative approach both fiscally and strategically. Frustrated and disappointed, feeling like they wanted to give up on the collaboration, they found a "CEO couples coach" to help them see if they could work through their differences. In their words, "we finally said all we needed to say" a process that felt like "renewing their vows."[1]

Immersion is another way of highlighting and exploring differences.[2] Rather than seeking a middle ground, the process of immersion enlists both people in delving into one person's expertise or perspective. It is a shared commitment to *temporarily* give up one person's "side" of the collaborative mix, to experience, as deeply as possible, the other "side." The purpose of immersion is to enhance our understanding of the other, not with the goal of surrendering our own views, but to expand what we can imagine is possible between us. Our potential for creating new insights or combinations is limited by the depth of our understanding of the other. Each of us will never be able to replicate what our collaborator brings to the work, but a deeper and more informed understanding of what they bring can contribute to creative tension.

The television program I referred to earlier in the book, *Undercover Boss*, is a powerful example of immersion as an approach to understanding differences. Each week the show revolved around a senior executive who took on a frontline job in their company. The executive was disguised, sometimes physically but always in terms of their identity. The immersion worked, in this case, because the "other," the cook or foreman or janitor or salesperson did not know that the "boss" was working with them. The deception allowed the boss to be immersed in the experience of the subordinate. In many cases, the bosses initially think they understand the subordinate's job. Some even worked the job "back in the day." Inevitably, however, the boss gains a deeper insight into the challenges their subordinates face on the job and the resourcefulness with which these challenges are addressed. Just as inevitably, the show ends with the bosses resolving to make changes because of their enlightening experience.

This show can be viewed as an entertaining exploration of a hierarchical collaboration. We can take some license in conceptualizing this relationship as a collaboration because both people depend upon each other to create something neither can accomplish alone. Their differences are profound and often can lead to tension, labor strife, and an uncomfortable if not toxic work environment. Even when both parties can appreciate each other's contribution to their shared task, their understanding, and thus their creativity, can be limited. In this show, the boss's immersion in the experience of the frontline worker led them to think differently about possible ways of organizing the work, approaches that were not in their field of vision before the immersion. One can only imagine what might surface for the boss and subordinate if a companion show, *Undercover Subordinate* could be envisioned and produced.

A story closer to me also illustrates the impact of immersion. Both Wells, my dear friend and colleague, and I appreciated each other's different backgrounds and prejudices. He was fond of poking fun at our respective ethnocentric attitudes, his as a Black man, mine as a White Jew. He was the first person I talked to about Black-Jewish relations. He had grown up in a town with a large Jewish population and he was one of the few people I could listen to, accept and engage when, for example, he started talking about the implications of Jewish "Chosen-ness." We had explored many difficult issues together, especially in our work with organizations on improving race relations.

After two decades of work together we created an immersion tool. We didn't use the term immersion at the time. We called it the Projective Intergroup Biographical Instrument (PIBI). The "instrument" involved two people swapping identities and then reporting their thoughts and feelings about inhabiting *what they imagined* were the identity characteristics of the other. As I began to imagine myself as a Black man, I learned both about my own projections onto Wells's life and simultaneously about my own background, specifically what I had internalized about Black men growing up White, male, Jewish, and middle class. From Leroy's reactions and questions, I learned more, both about myself and about him, especially about how he saw himself as a Black man. When I expressed rage and hopelessness, the first emotions that came to me as a "Black man," he told me that he understood, but that if that was all I could feel it would be a difficult and painful life. When we switched, I saw his view of White, Jewish men reflected in the privilege he felt and treasured with his temporary identity. He got to hear how I related (and didn't relate) to the status he attributed to me. We learned a great deal having thought we already knew a great deal. The immersion in each other's lives expanded our conversation about race and gender. It made possible new teaching, new thinking, and new work.

Conflict

Conflict has a bad reputation in the world of relationships, both personal and professional. A colleague of mine developed a decision-making heuristic that advised people in organizational leadership roles not to discuss an issue with a team if conflict was likely. In his model, conflict was an obstacle to effective team dynamics.[3] This is not an uncommon view of conflict. We are taught how to avoid conflict or how to resolve it. The emotions associated with conflict can distract us from the task. Dealing with conflict has even been described as a "process loss," that is, a waste of time.[4,5] A classic paper on group dynamics proposes four stages of development.[6] The second is "storming" and the fourth is "performing." The model strongly suggests that conflict is a necessary but problematic moment in a group's life to be gotten through in pursuit of effective functioning. Most of us enter a personal or professional relationship hoping that it will be conflict-free.

Yet experience teaches us that conflict is a familiar part of almost all relationships.[6] Think of any meaningful relationship you are in. Has there never been any conflict? The question makes no sense. Any relationship that has lasted long enough to become important has had moments or periods of conflict. Conflict is not an aberration in relationships, quite the opposite. When a friend tells you that their parents never fought, the idea is inconceivable to most of us. (It is more likely that the friend never *witnessed* their parents having a fight than that conflict never existed.) Conflict is both common and normal in relationships and collaborations are no exception.[7]

Conflict is how differences are surfaced, explored, and worked through. Conflict is often how we come to know ourselves and the other person more deeply. Conflict signals that something matters to us. We may not always be aware of how much something matters to us or to our collaborators until conflict occurs. The reason something matters to us can be clear and explicit (Who will get what percentage of the profits? Whose name will go first on the report?) or buried in the personal history of the collaborators ("I wasn't aware of it until now, but your tone of voice triggers something in me." "When you don't react to my idea, I feel dismissed."). In either case, we may have been ignoring what matters because we fear the consequences of serious disagreement. As a result, our first reaction to an incipient conflict is often to avoid it. The emotions involved when we are in conflict – anger, defensiveness, aggression, and pain – can be uncomfortable. At home, school, or in previous relationships we may have been advised to avoid them. And the wish to avoid these feelings could be rooted in the wish to avoid the possibility of confronting parts of ourselves and parts of the other that we might not like. But, avoiding conflict, like avoiding differences, can result in losing its potential benefits for the collaborative work.

Hesketh describes a conflict between Sullivan and Gilbert that almost ended their relationship.

> Sullivan said that his music was becoming repetitive and that his work had been dominated by Gilbert's words. He wanted more freedom; he wanted his music to speak for itself... Gilbert then wrote suggesting that Sullivan do his next opera with someone else. The quarrel *[that ensued]* had cleared the air and in an atmosphere of goodwill and serenity the partners produced a work that was the perfect expression of their artistic harmony *[what would become The Mikado]*.[8]

This event in their collaboration describes the forces driving the two men apart, the wish for separation and the threat of working with someone else. But in this case, the collaborators, like Sean and Emily, decided to have it out. The clearing of the air seems to have enabled the relationship to continue, creatively and productively.

Conflict often helps deepen a collaborative relationship. If we can tolerate the emotional heat often generated by conflict, we can learn about our collaborators. Conflict alerts us to the *stake* our collaborator has in the issue, not just their opinion or viewpoint. It can also alert us to our stake in an issue. How many of us have said, in the moment or upon reflection, "I didn't realize I felt that strongly about it" or "I didn't realize how strongly you felt about it" after a conflict with a colleague, friend, or family member? When we understand how strongly our collaborator feels, it can change how we listen to them and how we work with what they bring up.

Conflict can also contribute to the development of trust between collaborators. When we say that someone "pushed our button" we are referring to a source of *interpersonal* conflict located inside the *individual*. I can push your button intentionally or quite accidentally. In both cases, your response (and the conflict that can ensue) often reveals an insecurity or psychological vulnerability. We acknowledge as much when we admit the existence of a psychological button. The same comment might not have led to an angry or hurt response in someone else, but our personal history sensitizes us to certain words or actions, often leading to some form of conflict (passive or aggressive). Again, this kind of interaction can be painful and is often avoided, but when it happens there is also an opportunity, nested within the pain, for empathy and understanding. Trust develops between two people when vulnerability is revealed and not exploited, when a weakness or psychological "soft spot" is glimpsed in the other and we do not criticize or demean it. When our collaborator sees our limitations, and they inevitably will in the give and take of a collaboration and do not poke at them or bring them up later to score points, trust is built. Trust allows for more disclosure and more risk, necessary ingredients in a collaboration. Conflict can be an invaluable opportunity to develop this trust.[9]

Much has been written and taught about managing interpersonal conflict. The advice on how to have difficult conversations and how to move from entrenched positions to mutually beneficial solutions can be helpful when conflict occurs between collaborators.[9,10,11] As important as tools and concrete approaches are, our mindset about conflict in relationships is critical. Relationships do not grow or deepen without conflict. This is both an empirical fact and an intuitive truth. We can, if we choose, anticipate conflict at or near the beginning of a relationship. Instead of hoping that we will never have any conflicts, we can actively talk about, from what we know of ourselves and the other, what conflicts might arise as we work intensively and intimately with each other. Odd as this suggestion seems, it is surprising how much two people can identify about potential conflicts if they take the time to reflect on the topic. Anticipating conflict can inoculate us against the impulse to avoid it. We might recognize a conflict from our initial inventory rather than be taken by surprise when it shows up. This bit of familiarity can allow us to engage the conflict.

Engagement, the willingness to express and explore intense differences of opinion or feeling, is the key to managing conflict productively. When we feel a potential conflict, pushing the feeling aside or explaining it away does not help a collaboration. When a conflict occurs, running from it by withdrawing or counterattacking does not help the collaboration. The avoidance of conflict sets in motion a time bomb at the heart of a collaboration. Eventually, it will explode, it is very difficult to commit to raising conflicts and seeing them through, but no single commitment is more important to a sustainable collaboration. As we have reiterated many times, difference is the foundation of collaboration. It is also the source of most internal conflicts.

Competition

Collaboration always involves some competition. Striving together is part of joint creative work. We push each other to think differently in ways that we had not previously done. Our relationship takes us to levels of creative performance that we could not achieve alone. In contrast to working alone, collaboration involves reacting to the other. Without their words or actions, nothing much happens. Competition is similar in this way. It cannot happen without the other and it happens best, for the participants and for those invested in their contest when the competitors are raising each other's level of performance. In most competitions, however, the similarity to collaboration is submerged in the win/lose nature of the striving. The "winner" gets the promotion or the raise or the prize. The "loser" gets less or nothing. Lost is the relationship between the winner's performance and the loser's effort. Astute observers of a competition will notice that the quality of the competition was an indication of how the two contestants pushed each other. But the winning and losing aspect of competition understandably pushes an awareness and appreciation of this fact to the background.

In the give and take of collaboration, feelings of winning and losing can emerge. When the other person's idea moves our collective thinking forward, we can feel that we have lost in that moment. Or when the other's strengths are driving one piece of the work, we can forget that there are other pieces, pieces to which we have contributed, and we can feel like a runner-up. Collaboration involves shifting subordination, the capacity of the pair to defer to the strengths or insights of one and then the other without recourse to formal hierarchy or history, and without contesting the other simply for the sake of feeling like a winner (or avoiding feeling like a loser). Developing this capacity often means doing *something* with the feelings of winning and losing. If denied, these feelings can show up in the work itself, we may start to argue or disagree to rid ourselves of them. How can a collaboration metabolize competitive feelings in the service of the shared endeavor?

One approach is to emphasize the playful nature of competition. Play does not mean fanciful; it can allow the collaborators to take the feelings into a separate domain where they can "play out" separately from the work. When Smith and I wrote together the process was stressful because of our different styles. One of us would hold a pad and pen and take dictation. Later we would switch roles. The problem was that when I had the pen, I would constantly stop Smith from dictating to ask about word choice or sequence of ideas. Smith, with both restraint and frustration, would tell me to "Just write!" Editing would come later. When it was my turn to dictate, I would pace the room for long stretches of time before uttering a word, composing the entire outline of my thoughts before constructing the first sentence. Smith, again with both admirable restraint and frustration, would tell me "Just speak!" We would, he assured me, edit later. The different styles, the switching, and the frustration turned out not to be a problem. We laughed about it, worked our way through it, and wrote. The problem was how we felt after an afternoon of back and forth.

When Smith thought that our way of working vindicated his approach ("Look how much we have written today!") he felt good, and I felt as if

I had lost. When I thought we had produced work that needed minimal revision albeit with fewer pages to show for our effort, I felt good, and Smith felt as if he had lost. In the beginning, we were not conscious of this dynamic, of the feelings stirred by our collaboration. But we evolved a way of dealing with the feelings, nonetheless: we played handball in Smith's basement at the end of each working session. The playful, intense game, made up on the spot to include legal (and illegal) bounces off the oil burner and clothes dryer, provided an outlet for the competitive aspect of our collaboration. Not always, but often, the person who felt as if they had "lost" in our writing process that day "won" at handball. Neither of us was conscious of throwing the game. On the contrary, the rivalry was full throttle. But later, reflecting on how we created and implemented the game, we were struck by the equilibrium maintained by the competition at day's end. It is rare that collaborations can exist for an extended period without addressing the competitive feelings generated by joint work. Finding a playful way to express and manage these feelings helps collaborators stay connected.

Stories emerged from the Obama White House about basketball games to which the president would invite friends who were casual basketball players as well as former college athletes. The games were reported as hard-fought. It was also reported that Obama chose the best players for his team and that, not surprisingly, his team often won. Perhaps President Obama liked to win because he was competitive. But my interpretation of these reports is different. I imagine Obama struggled every day to collaborate with "different" others (both inside his party and with some from the other side) in the service of a political agenda. He articulated this aspiration when he took office. I also imagine that he felt as if he were losing in these efforts to collaborate on most days. Perhaps the basketball games, stacked to allow the president to "win," were a way of managing the competition that was always present in his efforts at political collaboration.[12]

Limitations

Gilbert is quoted as saying, "I know my limitations and capabilities better than anyone else. No man is successful until he learns that lesson."[13] In true Gilbert fashion, the quote is a bit over the top and may even deconstruct itself, but the observation about the role of understanding one's limitations in a successful collaboration is spot on. A key challenge for collaborators is the acceptance of their own limitations and weaknesses. As we have noted, the challenge of integrating the shadow, the aspects of the self that we would prefer to disown or, failing that, hide away somewhere out of sight can be daunting. Ironically, the urge to hide these unwanted parts increases with the closeness of the relationship. The more intimate the connection, the more we wish to hide aspects of the self that might "ruin" this important relationship. Since we reject these characteristics, we assume that others will reject them too. The urge to hide, cover, not bring up, or even deny our limitations and weaknesses is universal unless we choose to explore these shadowy aspects out of necessity (e.g., the pain they cause us) or curiosity (e.g., a 360-degree review of our performance).

Accepting our limitations may seem a laudable goal in general and an important one for collaborative success but we are taught throughout life to improve on our limitations. Getting better at schoolwork or sports, working on our weaknesses, and improving our public speaking are exhortations that make explicit the goal of minimizing or eliminating our limitations. No child is encouraged to accept their limitations because childhood is about developing a wide range of abilities all of which begin as a limitation. The consequence of these necessary exhortations is a deep-seated resistance to accepting limitations in the service of collaborative work. When we are in an intimate relationship with someone whose skill, talent, and background exceed ours (as relates to our shared task) resistance to accepting our limitations can seriously impair our ability to work together. My *internal* struggle to improve upon my limitations can become an *external* struggle with my collaborator. "Proving" that I am competent or that I am "im-proving" to become competent can be inefficient at best (let Sally do it, she's better at it) and a source of difficult and persistent conflict at worst (how come you argue with me about *my* area of expertise.) Accepting my limitations means accepting your possibilities.

Acceptance of limitations in a collaboration translates into a regular interaction with someone who reminds us of what we (and in many cases the world in which we live and work) would rather avoid. Every time we collaborate, we stare across the room at someone whose strengths complement ours (that's the good news) and simultaneously point to our weaknesses (that's the challenge). If we cannot accept our limitations, we may find ourselves avoiding these working sessions without understanding why. Our avoidance may be a way of stepping out of a relationship that subtly, even unconsciously, tells us that we should be better.

In most organizations, it is not simply the strengths of my collaborator that may trigger my insecurities about my limitations and weaknesses. The organization itself is committed to my "continuous improvement" not my selective acceptance of limitations. When, as part of a leadership development course, I distribute a 360-degree survey to my bosses, peers, and subordinates I receive a report once the anonymous surveys are returned and compiled. The report presents me (usually within the first few pages) with my strengths and my "areas for improvement." The implication is clear. The goal for the 20 or 30 behavioral dimensions of effective leadership is perfection. I would be a model employee if I had the highest rating on all the dimensions. Stepping back from this increasingly ubiquitous exercise it is obvious that encouraging human beings to be perfect flies in the face of reality. A report that cannot even use the word "weaknesses," to say nothing of describing a rationale for *accepting* these weaknesses, reinforces our belief that limitations and weaknesses are liabilities for our organizational roles.

They are not. Our limitations make collaborations possible. Imagine this alternative reality. A cover page for a 360-degree survey says:

> In the pages that follow you will find a summary of how others perceive your strengths and weaknesses. In some cases, we will advise you to keep developing your strengths (e.g., results orientation, commitment to the development of subordinates). In other cases, we will advise you to improve in certain areas where a certain level of competence is required in our work (e.g., honesty, understanding of HR resources for employees in crisis). In still other cases we will advise you to accept your limitations and seek out someone to add to your team who complements your deficiency with competence and expertise. We believe that such a relationship has the potential to make a greater contribution to the organization than asking either of you to spend time and effort on your weaknesses (and away from your strengths). This advice has some teeth to it. We will resurvey you and your immediate collaborators (peers and subordinates) in one year. If their profiles do not suggest significant complementarity with your own, we'll want to know why. If they do represent significant complementarity, we will look at the kind of working environment you have been able to create to see if these collaborators feel able to express their difference inside your relationship. If they do not, we will want to know why.

Even as a thought experiment, we can imagine what would happen with this kind of an introduction to a 360-degree survey. Instead of focusing on our *individual* plan for the next year, largely focused on maintaining "good" ratings and improving "bad" ones, our focus shifts to a "relationship" plan. How do I attract and retain people who complement my strengths? In this scenario, the survey *helps* with my acceptance of limitations by instructing me about them and, more importantly, by contextualizing them as beneficial to the work of my organization. It supports that explanation with suggestions for how to move forward (because everyone has limitations and can move forward *with* them not in denial *about* them) and with descriptions of the consequences of an inability to move forward as suggested.

There are two practical keys to the acceptance of my limitations while in a relationship. The first is that my limitations (and presumably my collaborator's as well) must become an acceptable part of the relationship. If my weaknesses are ridiculed or critically pointed out, I will defend or I will withdraw. If my weaknesses are appreciated or acknowledged because they make room for the strengths of my partner, my personal acceptance grows. When the collaboration between Rosso and Lukins was working, Rosso's limitations as a "cook" were accepted and acknowledged as were Lukins's limitations in media relations and promotional activity. When the collaboration became strained, these same limitations became instruments of attack further jeopardizing the relationship.

The second key to accepting one's limitations is illustrated in the following example. Recently a friend reported to me that among the commitments a couple made to each other at a recent wedding was this one. "I promise to continue my therapy, because we will only be successful if I keep working on myself." This is a remarkable statement when made in public (most public commitment ceremonies only allude to the difficulties of maintaining the relationship). It articulates the connection between relational success and individual work. In this case, the therapeutic work involves continuous attention to integrating the shadow, to exploring one's "limitations" and, rather than always "fixing" them or avoiding them, integrating them into our own self-understanding so that when our partner notices them or stumbles onto them, we do not run or fight in response. Pema Chodoron might call this regularly inviting your demons to tea.[14] Acceptance of our limitations is not a one-time thing. The task is best seen as a lifetime's work.

Dealing with the World

As we have discussed, all collaborations exist in a context. Work collaborations involve transactions with this context. The collaboration's product is sold, presented, or offered to the world in which the collaboration is embedded. The product could be something physical and concrete like a prototype of a new mousetrap or an operetta complete with lyrics and score. Someone needs to invest in the mousetrap, produce it, and sell it. And someone needs to produce the operetta, promote it, and encourage people to come see it. Collaborations also produce ideas or concepts that are presented or "pitched" to the world around the collaboration, a boss or a committee. Without the needs and desires of the environment, many collaborations would not exist. If no one needed to trap a mouse, there would be no pressure to invent a mousetrap. If no one appreciated and yearned for musical theater, there might be little press for operettas.

The environment has different connections to the collaborative relationship and to each of the collaborators. The groups from which collaborators come may have different interests in the collaborative effort. The interest could be emotional, a wish for success or failure, rooted in the consequences for the group of the collaboration (e.g., a marriage across religious or ethnic backgrounds encouraged or forbidden by the families of the two people involved), or quite practical, rooted in the investment a group has made in the collaboration (e.g., the publishing house of an editor who signs a writer to a book contract). We have also discussed the ways in which the world outside the collaboration reacts to these relationships, often finding it difficult to relate to the *pair* in doling out credit, reward, criticism, or advice. The result, often, is that the collaboration can be stretched or pulled apart by the needs, wants, and practices of the world around it.

Managing these outside groups and pressures is a two-person job. It may seem to be the responsibility of one or the other collaborator, especially when the pressure is coming from their "side" of the relationship. If my family is unhappy about my romantic relationship, isn't it my responsibility to manage that? If you convinced the finance committee to authorize seed money for our project, isn't it your job to manage the anxieties of the finance people? If the company gave me a bonus for our joint work but not you, whose job is it to point that out? In all these cases and many more, the *approach* to handling the situation is the responsibility of both collaborators even if the *implementation* of that approach is done by one or the other person. The reason for this suggestion is that handling the external world is much like the collaboration itself. There is a greater likelihood of an effective solution to the problem when both collaborators participate in creating the approach. The "closeness" of one collaborator may be balanced by the "removed" perspective of the other. The reactions of one collaborator's "home" group may not be as troublesome or disturbing to the other collaborator given their relative lack of historical connection to the group.

A few examples will serve to illustrate the role of both collaborators in managing the external forces acting on them. First, a cross-department collaboration involving a representative from each department required the two collaborators to manage a complex process whereby each of their departments would consider a new proposal. The collaborators wanted to minimize the influence of the historical baggage carried by both groups on the discussions. The collaboration itself had all the dynamics described above. Each collaborator brought their department's perspective to the project. As they worked together, the two people had to learn to listen to, trust, and engage these differences in the service of their joint task. As they got closer to creating a workable proposal that neither thought possible when they began, it became clear that the acceptance of the proposal by their respective departments depended not simply on the quality of the proposal, but also on how it was presented to each department. Instead of defaulting to each collaborator presenting the proposal to their respective department, the two designed an approach in which each collaborator presented to the "other" department but only after being introduced and accompanied by the "home" group collaborator. The idea was based on their shared belief that the home departments would be more able to hear the proposal (and less likely to criticize it reflexively) if it were presented by the "outsider" but only if there was public and consistent support from the "inside" collaborator. The proposals still elicited feedback, and the collaboration worked through many revisions, but this continued collaborative work was made possible by a thoughtful and agreed-upon approach created by the two collaborators as they faced the challenges of their embedded situation.

Second, Tony and Jenny, the coaching collaboration that had been working together for years, discovered a pay differential. Jenny was being paid significantly less than she deserved (less, in fact, than more junior coaches on the men's side of the sport). In their relationship, Jenny was the one who historically handled the "administrative" aspects of their job. She was the interface with the administration in securing resources for the team. She was described by Tony as the "tough one." But on this issue, the two decided that Tony would implement their approach to the pay differential, an inequality that threatened the collaboration's future. (He was quite upset about the inequity and happy to push the issue forcefully.) Since the pay differential itself symbolized the general regard for women coaches, Tony told the Athletic Director that *he* would be leaving if *she* didn't receive an equitable salary. Perhaps if Jenny had said she would leave without equitable pay, the administration might have been responsive as well. But the collaborative pair decided that the best way to handle this external "threat" to their continued work together was to have a senior man talk to senior men about gender inequity in pay. The lesson is less about the actual approach and more about the fact that the pair worked on it together rather than leaving the issue to one of them, in this case, the female, underpaid coach.[15]

The third example returns us to Molly and Sabrina, the administrator-faculty pair working together on a program to support inclusion and belonging on a college campus. As a collaboration across multiple organizational and identity groups, Molly and Sabrina were regularly confronted with the needs and interests of their home groups. There was always the risk to Sabrina, for example, that the Black community and the faculty community might see her as "selling out" to the White administration's agenda. Molly too faced potential criticism from members of her "constituencies" who disagreed with the resources being devoted to the initiative. If these relations with the world surrounding their collaboration were not handled well, the relationship between Molly and Sabrina would be jeopardized, and if that happened the program to which they were both committed would also be in trouble.

Throughout their collaboration they agreed to work together to help each other manage their respective relationships with the outside communities they represented. This was never easy. The tensions on the campus, especially tensions that involved faculty and administration found their way into the relationship between Molly and Sabrina. As a result, their relationship was often tense. But they were committed to working on these tensions together. Sabrina might be the one to speak to Black faculty about the administration's support (or perceived lack of support) for certain aspects of the initiative, but the content of her side of the conversation was discussed together. Molly might be the one to speak to the Board, but what she said and how she presented the initiative was discussed, and sometimes argued about, by the two of them.

The broader suggestion for how to manage these external factors is that the collaborative pair make an explicit psychological contract early in their relationship and revisit it often.[16] A psychological contract is an articulation of the expectations of the two people involved for the working relationship and an agreement on the process by which, together, they will address instances in which those expectations are not being met. In a work collaboration, such a contract includes an upfront discussion of how the joint work will be credited, how any rewards, financial or organizational will be shared, how the collaboration will be publicly acknowledged, how the respective time investments will be accounted for in the decisions on credit, reward, and acknowledgment. It is also a commitment to bring the effects of external events to the collaborative relationship even if they are experienced by only one of the collaborators. This allows the pair to help each other manage these external events and their impact on the relationship.

This psychological contract is constantly being revisited. As the two people involved learn about each other and about their own desires and expectations, both of which are likely to change over time, the shared understating which is the heart of the "contract" will need updating. Not only will the two people need to let each other know what is changing in their personal and professional lives that is relevant to their shared work (e.g., increasing financial obligations, increasing time commitments at home or on other projects, decreasing interest in this work, imminent promotion decision) but they also need to discuss the implications of these changes for their agreed-upon working arrangement (e.g., financial and reputational benefits, timeline to completion). The relationship also evolves in the face of success and failure, and as the world around the collaboration makes ever-changing demands on it. A collaborative pair is wise to check in on their psychological contract. This is the routine maintenance on the collaborative machine. Check the contract every month, whether you think you need to or not. When you defer routine maintenance, you risk severe damage to the relationship.

Endnotes

1 Personal interview.
2 David N. Berg and Kenwyn K. Smith, *Paradoxes of Group Life: Understanding Conflict, Paralysis, and Movement in Group Dynamics* (San Francisco, CA: Jossey-Bass, 1987).
3 Victor H. Vroom and Phillip W. Yetton, *Leadership and Decision-Making* (Pittsburgh, PA: University of Pittsburgh Press, 1973).
4 J. Richard Hackman and Charles G. Morris, '1Group Tasks, Group Interaction Process, and Group Performance Effectiveness: A Review and Proposed Integration,' *Advances in Experimental Social Psychology* 8 (1975): 45–99.
5 Latané, Bibb, Kipling Williams, and Stephen Harkins, 'Many Hands Make Light the Work: The Causes and Consequences of Social Loafing,' *Journal of Personality and Social Psychology* 37, no. 6 (1979): 822–832.
6 Bruce W. Tuckman, 'Developmental Sequence in Small Groups,' *Psychological Bulletin* 63, no. 6 (1965): 384–399.
7 David N. Berg and Kenwyn K. Smith, *Paradoxes of Group Life: Understanding Conflict, Paralysis, and Movement in Group Dynamics* (San Francisco, CA: Jossey-Bass, 1987).
8 Hesketh Pearson, *Gilbert and Sullivan: A Biography* (New York: Harper & Row, 1935).
9 Lauren Taylor and David N. Berg, 'The Challenge of Mutual Disclosure in Global Health Partnerships,' *Perspectives in Biology and Medicine* 62, no. 4 (2019): 657–673.
10 Robert E. Walton, *Interpersonal Peacemaking: Confrontations and Third-Party Consultation* (Reading, MA: Addison-Wesley 1972).
11 Douglas Stone, Sheila Heen, and Bruce Patton, *Difficult Conversations: How to Discuss What Matters Most* (London: Penguin, 2023).
12 Roger Fisher and William Ury, *Getting to Yes: Negotiating Agreement Without Giving in* (London: Penguin, 2011).
13 Hesketh Pearson, *Gilbert and Sullivan: A Biography* (New York: Harper & Row, 1935).
14 Pema Chödrön, *When Things Fall Apart: Heart Advice for Difficult Times* (Boulder, CO: Shambhala Publications, 2000).
15 Personal interview.
16 Denise M. Rousseau, 'The 'Problem' of the Psychological Contract Considered,' *Journal of Organizational Behavior* 19, no. S1 (1998): 665–671.

Chapter 10

Getting Out, Being Apart

The urge to separate, to move away from a collaborative relationship, is common. Its frequency points to its function in maintaining the collaboration. The suggestion that moving apart is necessary for the long-term success of a collaboration may seem counterintuitive, but by this point in this book, the explanations for the role of separation in an intense collaboration will be familiar. In Chapter 7, we discussed how the complementary differences that make the collaboration creative and productive can attenuate over time. The more two people work together, the more they are likely to begin to see their task in similar terms. The collaborative relationship becomes an integral part of each person's identity. Increasingly, over time, the collaborative relationship becomes like their other group memberships. The more time they spend together, the more shared experiences they generate and the more the shared understandings of those experiences become part of each person's perspective. If, for example, a marketing professional and a product specialist are working together on rolling out a promotional plan, the more they jointly develop ideas and adopt them, the more similar their next approach to idea generation will be. In addition to the professional and personal *differences* they brought to the collaboration, they are now building a *common* repertoire of ideas and approaches. This common repertoire is a product of the collaboration and often moves the collaboration forward in creative and productive ways, but it can also begin to supplant the different perspectives each collaborator originally brought to the relationship. They may not be aware of this growing commonality until they notice themselves struggling to develop new ideas. When a creative relationship gets "stale," it may be because the areas of shared commonality have become larger than the areas of difference.

Return and Replenish

When this happens, one or both collaborators may feel the need to "return to their roots," to the environment that nourished their skill set or

DOI: 10.4324/9781032701998-10

perspective. The longer they have been inside the collaboration, the more they may feel that their communities of origin, professional or personal, have evolved. They may feel out of touch with the latest developments in their field or out of practice having not done "pure" work in their chosen field or with people whose specialty is theirs. Rosso and Lukins put it succinctly, they each wanted to get back to their own kitchens.[1] The desire to move away from the collaboration and toward the places from which they come may stem from a wish to reconnect with these personal or professional identities. The years that contribute skills and perspectives to the collaboration also shape our identities. I am a psychologist because of the decades of study and practice that have been a part of my life. But the longer I am away from psychology, the less I feel like a psychologist and the more I seek out opportunities to be with this important and foundational group. The conversations and discussions, even the jokes and gossip within my "group" feel comfortable and affirming. They may also stimulate me in ways that discussions and conversations with non-psychologists cannot.

While this reconnection takes me away from my collaboration, it also can be an investment in it. A research scientist who has been collaborating with a pharmaceutical industry representative to develop new drug therapies for a disease will, over time, begin to understand and consider the needs of a for-profit company. If they are paid for their time, the financial benefit derived from this collaboration can further cement the relationship. The collaboration works, in part, because the scientist becomes increasingly knowledgeable about how a private sector company operates, and the company representative learns more deeply about the science and the ethics of academic research. This "identification" with the private sector takes the scientist away from the academic community. Similarly, an understanding of the realities of academic medicine may alienate the company representative from the business functions of finance and marketing. But ultimately, the collaboration becomes less useful to both parties if the scientist becomes alienated from their scientific community, or the company representative fails to give voice to the interests of their organization.

The scientist's desire to reconnect with their colleagues, colleagues who may even question their involvement with industry, can be understood as a desire to be back in intimate touch with the professional identity that made them valuable as a collaborator. A scientist who "collaborates" with industry often worries about how they will be viewed by the scientific research community. Reconnecting with that community strengthens the scientist's standing, both professional and psychological, with their scientific colleagues. The company representative, like the scientist, must remain connected to the core mission of their organization to hold up their end of the collaboration. The private company has been successful at bringing therapies to market because it has been able to market and promote these therapies better than or as well as their competitors. Regular attendance at profit and loss meetings where the goals and practices of their company are reinforced, even in the face of the scientist's views and opinions, is crucial to the company representative remaining credible in their own organization.

Reconnection with home groups or core identities is a vehicle for psychological and professional replenishment. When my first job took me from a psychology department to a school of management, I was acutely aware that terms like "boilerplate" and "bottom line" were foreign to me. I had to ask my colleagues from the business world, in whispered asides, to define these terms for me! Five years later, having worked with these same colleagues to create a learning environment for management students, I found myself using the same terms. Using "business" terms facilitated my collaboration in many ways, but it also meant that the psychologist's view was slowly disappearing. What is the impact of relationships in corporations of using "boilerplate" language in a memo or email? What might be the implications for the culture of a public or not-for-profit organization of adopting the language of economics to describe work relationships in organizations? Periodically reconnecting with my psychological colleagues by attending conferences or writing papers, made it more likely that I could and would ask these questions. Asking the questions made my contribution to the discussion of management education more valuable even when the questions were troubling to my collaborators.

The second explanation for why one or both collaborators want to move away from the intensity of the relationship is because they feel they are losing themselves in the collaboration. The collaboration, by its success (e.g., the names of the two collaborators are always said in one breath) or by its internal dynamics (e.g., neither person can think of doing work without the other) has begun to erase the individuals whose separate and distinct characters gave birth to the collaboration in the first place. This loss of individual identity in the relationship threatens each person's integrity (wholeness) and the potential for the relationship to form a connection across differences, differences which are at risk of being overwhelmed, paradoxically, by the intensity of the connection.

The Drama of Embrace

Miroslav Volf is a Christian theologian who was born in communist Yugoslavia and watched as the Balkans exploded in the 1990s. He was Croatian by birth but grew up in a predominantly Serbian community. Much of his work centers on how people with different identities, especially when those identities have been involved in conflict, can find a way to make a relationship of caring and compassion. We have characterized collaborations as connections across difference. In his book *Exclusion and Embrace* [2] Volf uses the metaphor of an "embrace" to describe such a relationship, one that simultaneously respects the individuality of the other person while inviting them into an intimate connection. The four stages of what Volf calls the "drama of embrace" are worth examining because they capture, albeit in a different language, the essence of a collaborative relationship. The final stage, "letting go" is of particular interest to us in this chapter on the role of separation in a collaboration.

Volf proposes four elements to an embrace: opening the arms, waiting, closing the arms, and opening them again. Akin to the idea that collaboration (embrace) is predicated on the limitations of each collaborator, Volf suggests that "non-self-sufficiency" is at the heart of this first element. The welcoming of the other is created by the *need* for the other person. Like a collaboration, the first act is an attraction to the other based on a desire for what the other brings. This welcome is enacted by an invitation to come in, with open arms (rather than judgment or suspicion) that draws the other into the possibilities of a relationship. The second element also resonates with the collaborative relationship. Waiting is an expression of the non-coercive nature of a genuine embrace. It signals that one person is open to a relationship but only if it is also desired by the other. In the language of collaboration, waiting can be understood as the exploration of difference that results in the mutual decision to collaborate. The third element is the closing of the arms, arguably the element of an embrace that most quickly comes to mind when we think of a hug since there is no hug without closing the arms. But Volf emphasizes the mutual nature of this element as well. Both people must close their arms to make an embrace and yet both people must also be able to receive the gentle squeeze from the other. Closing the arms can be likened to elements of the collaborative relationship discussed earlier: listening to, accepting, and engaging the other while simultaneously expressing oneself in hopes of mutual acceptance and engagement.

It is the fourth element of the embrace that addresses the dynamics of separation. Volf sees the opening of the arms again not as the end of the embrace but as a part of it. Here's how Volf describes the necessity of letting go:

> What holds the *[two people]* together in an embrace is not their welded boundary, but the arms placed around each other. And if the embrace is not to cancel itself, the arms must open again. Were this not to happen, embrace would signal the final 'disappearance of the "I" into the "we." As the final act of the embrace, the opening of the arms underlines that, though the other may be inscribed into the self … the other

> may not be neutralized by merging both into an undifferentiated "we." The other must be let go so that ... her genuine dynamic identity may be preserved; and the self must take itself back into itself so that its own identity, enriched by the traces that the presence the other has left, may be preserved. The other must be let go, finally, so that "the negotiation of difference" which can "never produce a final settlement," may be continued. (Walzer, 1994, p. 83)[3]

In the language of collaboration, letting go provides an antidote to the risk of a relationship that fuses two identities into one, a relationship that erases the individual differences at the center of a collaboration. Letting go, when it is mutual, also allows the collaborative relationship to assert the importance of the individual identities of the two people involved, releasing them, at least temporarily, into these separate and independent selves. Volf's conceptualization of the embrace makes separation a necessary part of a respectful, mutually engaged, and reciprocal relationship. A productive collaboration strives to be all of these. Separation is a necessary part of collaboration. Why then is separation not often seen as part of a collaborative relationship? Why, in fact, is it often seen as evidence of a failed collaboration?

Why Is Separation So Difficult?

A relationship that needs to be together to succeed can struggle with the importance of being apart. A move by one person to take time alone or to seek temporary separation can feel like a rejection of the other person. The closer the collaborative relationship, the more likely movement away can be upsetting to the person "left behind." Separation evokes feelings of betrayal or abandonment. The intimacy and vulnerability that allow collaborations to work can make separation painful or confusing. Collaborators can wonder what went wrong or what they must have done to drive the other away. Or they can project their fears about having alienated their partner, blaming them instead for the choice to withdraw. One way to soothe feelings of rejection and abandonment is to find reasons to reject the other. Remember when hurt by Sullivan's critique of their collaborative work and his desire to get away from the relationship, Gilbert suggests he work with someone else? Go, be gone, I don't want to work with you either![4]

Releasing an embrace can be awkward even in a casual setting. Who lets go first? Will a release of the hug be interpreted as a wish to break the embrace or as discomfort with the intimacy of the embrace? But an embrace cannot go on forever, so how do we signal to each other that the embrace has ended without evoking unintended emotional messages? If we mix up these messages, the feelings that attend the first movement away, the opening of the arms to let go, can cause the other to hold on tighter. We are leaving home for college, or a first job and we embrace our parent to say goodbye. The embrace is not a simple one since it carries the history of the parent-child relationship that now must evolve to allow both people to let go. Both people must move on so that they can move back together later, as adults. Like the separation in collaboration, this leave-taking is necessary. It is an important part of the parent-child relationship, and it can feel like the end of a relationship rather than a part of one. At that moment one of the two can feel the urge to hold on, if only for a few more seconds, in the face of the impending, inevitable, and necessary separation.

Necessary Separations

In the face of the emotions stirred by separation, it can be challenging for any collaboration to find ways to incorporate this necessary dimension into the relationship. In its simplest and most easily implemented form, the challenge is met by the logistics of the relationship. Pauses in the work or breaks from the intensity of collaboration are built into the working relationship. The two people involved may not live in the same place or may work in different departments. The collaborative project may be only one of their many work responsibilities and therefore only a fraction of their daily face-to-face time. The work itself may include periods of separation, times when each of the collaborators is working on a piece of the joint endeavor, writing a first draft, constructing a prototype, contacting other sources, or running an experiment. Coach Jenny talked about what she would do when Tony got on her nerves. She would simply schedule a recruiting trip, time away from campus (and from Tony). Because it was self-scheduled, Jenny could use this aspect of the work to manage their needed separation. These naturally occurring breaks serve the purpose of separation by giving the collaborators time to recharge themselves, reconnect to other parts of their lives or simply step back from the intensity of the creative process.[4]

Sean and Emily were scared about their growing separation. They had founded the business together. As Sean put it, "We were complete as a partnership. Incomplete alone." Facing economic challenges during the COVID pandemic and butting up against their different ways of responding to this crisis they confronted the tensions and were able to work them through. And the "logistics" of their lives helped. Part of working through the tensions involved giving each other time apart. By luck and circumstance, their living arrangements changed, and they no longer live in the same city. Adapting to working remotely actually helped turn down the intensity in their relationship thereby preserving it.[5]

It can be helpful for collaborations to develop ways of separating that are emotionally acceptable to both people when the structure of their work together does not easily support such separation. "Separate vacations" is a ritualistic way of putting separation in a relationship. Jenny likened her decades-long collaboration with Tony to a marriage with separate vacations. Too much uninterrupted time together would have ruined the collaboration. But the metaphor of separate vacations requires the two people to "contract" for this respite and regeneration. As a child, I heard about other people's parents having separate vacations and thought it strange. Why marry someone and then take separate vacations? Now in my fifth decade of marriage, I understand this mutual choice differently. Separate vacations do not necessarily mean estrangement or rejection. Now, in the context of collaboration, I understand them as ritualistic periods of separation that have the potential to strengthen rather than weaken a relationship.

Other formal or ritualistic separations include "poker games," "book clubs," "sports nights," "roommate reunions," and "ski trips." These activities are both real and metaphoric, symbolizing the time *away* from a collaborative partner and *with* members of one's "home" groups. In professional settings, these home group meetings can be as simple as lunch with one's department or an educational event in one's area of expertise. They can also be an expression of one's need to be temporarily free of the behavioral norms and expectations of the groups to which your collaborator belongs. The development of "affinity" groups in organizations, groups of people from similar backgrounds, serves to give a voice to people who, individually, might feel too vulnerable to speak. It also, and not incidentally, provides a place that is free of the stress of discrimination, stereotyping, and micro-aggressions that are part of all interactions across groups like race, gender, ethnicity, and sexual orientation, collaborations being no exception.

Leroy Wells, who I introduced earlier, was my teaching assistant during my first major teaching assignment. We had developed a collaboration around teaching, especially around race relations, before our class began. As a White man and a Black man working together in front of a predominantly White group of management students in a predominantly White, elite academic institution we were both looking forward to creating a learning environment that included the topic of race relations in organizations. We met almost daily, prepared two classes a week together, and confronted the challenges of co-teaching. It felt intimate and creative to me. What I would now call a model collaboration.

Midway through the semester I was walking through a common room in the school and saw Wells sitting with a small group of Black students. I knew many of the students (there were only a handful of Black students in the entire program) and walked over to say hello. The reception I got felt a little chilly to me. I was the only White person in the gathering and the only faculty member. Within a few moments, the lighthearted banter began to focus on me, jokes at my expense and some increasingly sharp teasing comments. I was accustomed to this when in the company of students. Outside the classroom, I was fair game and usually took such teasing as a sign of a relatively comfortable relationship. In this case, I became increasingly distressed that Wells was joining the teasing, leaving me alone and isolated in the face of it. Eventually, I left the group feeling a bit betrayed and abandoned by my friend and colleague.

That night I had a dream that showed just how strong my unconscious reactions had been to this event. In the dream, I was on my knees and Wells was standing over me with a pistol, preparing to shoot. I woke up in a mild panic, fully aware that my encounter with the group of Black students had stirred something very deep. I recognized the racial trope of the violent Black man, buried but alive in my unconscious. I had projected that Wells was angry with me (when in fact, I was angry with him) and then fantasized that his anger would turn violent. This was not the real-life Wells. This was my unconscious. I called a White male colleague who had immersed himself in studying and trying to change race relations in this country and found myself expressing my disappointment that the relationship I thought I had with Wells did not exist. Why hadn't he defended me in front of the other Black students? We were intimate collaborators and yet he had left me to be teased by the Black students. Worse, he had joined in the teasing.

For me this was a lesson in the power and necessity of what we are calling "home groups." What my White colleague taught me that day was that Wells could be and needed to be both a Black student *and* a teaching collaborator with me. I had felt these two identities in conflict. Either Wells was loyal to me, or he was loyal to the other Black students. When he expressed his connection to the Black students, I felt he was betraying his connection to me. The truth about our relationship was that we were deeply connected to each other across our many differences, including race and hierarchical role, *and* we were deeply and importantly connected to groups outside our relationship. Not only were these multiple connections not in conflict, but they were also the lifeblood of our collaboration. Our work on race relations depended on each of us remaining connected to our racial identities. Our successful work as teachers depended on Wells maintaining a connection to students (of all backgrounds) and my maintaining my "status" as a professor with the authority to innovate and adapt in the classroom.

The feelings associated with this dramatic manifestation of our connections to our home groups (had I not been a White faculty member the teasing would have been quite different) obscured for *me* the importance of these connections. Given the history of race relations in this country and in higher education, the necessity of developing *both* authentic interpersonal relationships with faculty *and* maintaining the support of one's racial identity cohort was not news to Wells. When power differences are part of a collaboration, the collaborator from the more powerful societal group is likely to see the collaboration in strictly *interpersonal* terms the way I did. The collaborator from the less powerful societal group is likely to see the collaboration as *also* always involving *intergroup* relations.

Two lessons emerge for me as I reflect on this example of "betrayal" in a collaboration. The first centers on the *both/and* framing of the interpersonal and intergroup connections. When these connections are experienced as *either/or* the collaboration is endangered by a false choice. Since all of us are both individuals and members of groups, forcing ourselves to choose one aspect of our identity over another inevitably leads to a denial of one connection or another and to feelings of guilt and betrayal. The second lesson emphasizes the importance of the home group connection. Without regular contact with and connection to our home groups, the collaborative difference becomes effaced and its potential diminished. In the situation described above, the conversation that ensued between me and Wells following my telling him about the dream, deepened our relationship as I learned about the role of the Black student group in Wells's life and about my own unconscious racism, and he learned about his importance to me and the role of hierarchy in our "peer-like" collaboration.

Working with Others

The final and perhaps most difficult suggestion for managing separation in a collaboration is the important role played by each collaborator working with other people. Each member of a collaboration working with other people is both common and inevitable. It is rare that anyone collaborates with only one other person. Organizations frequently assign people to work with many different individuals and teams. Artists, performers, and musicians are constantly forming and dissolving collaborations. Scientific researchers and video game inventors also collaborate with different people depending upon the work being undertaken. And yet, the unremarkable action of Charlie working with Maria and then separately working with Rasheed is likely to stir emotions in Maria. In my own experience, I hesitate to bring up my exciting new collaborations with Smith for fear of hurting his feelings. This is undoubtedly my projection since my fear is based on how I feel when he tells me about his new collaborations. But this inhibition about "confessing" my outside work points to an emotional component to working outside a primary collaboration.

The inhibition, the withholding, makes the reality of outside working relationships more awkward and potentially more disruptive to the primary collaboration in two ways. First, the withholding is likely to increase my collaborator's suspicion when they find out. The suspicion is that I want out of our collaboration or that something about our collaboration is not right and I'm not telling them about it. Suspicion leads to mutual withholding and the essential, expressive nature of collaboration in which both people give voice to their often-differing thoughts and feelings is undermined. Second, the potential contribution of work outside the collaboration is that ideas, techniques, and solutions found in other relationships can be brought into the collaboration. Feeling inhibited about bringing up these other relationships can lead to withholding what has been learned from them.

Two examples from the world of music illustrate the importance of working with others as a way of being apart. The first example is a story that ends with the breakup of the collaboration, but not the end of each person's creative collaborations. The second example involves a long-term collaboration regularly enriched by each collaborator's work with others.

Much has been written in an effort to understand the collaboration between John Lennon and Paul McCartney. The Beatles included Ringo Starr and George Harrison, but most of their song catalog is jointly credited to Lennon and McCartney. The two men were different in some ways and similar in others. Their creativity is the stuff of musical legend. The breakup of the Beatles has also been a subject of much reporting, especially the breakup of Lennon and McCartney. In their own words, the breakup was an expression of their shared desire to be free of the "Beatles," a desire shared by all four members of the group. The Beatles had become more of a creative burden than a creative vehicle.[6,7] The identity of the Beatles had begun to stifle the identities of its members. They wanted out. For John Lennon, the way out involved a creative relationship with Yoko Ono.

For some devotees of the Beatles, it is tempting to cast Yoko Ono in the role of band-breaker. Neither Lennon nor McCartney saw it this way. Lennon's voice was less and less present in the songs they wrote together (by agreement all their songs were jointly credited for as long as the band existed) in the later years. When Lennon started to work with Yoko Ono, the collaboration brought back an edgy kind of creativity that had ebbed away in his work with McCartney and the Beatles. As noted in Chapter 7, neither man saw Yoko Ono as the cause of their separation, a work separation that lasted until Lennon's death. Ono did represent the movement away from a collaboration that had begun to stifle their individual creativity. Both men needed to get out of their very productive relationship to continue as creative artists. McCartney too went on to form his own new artistic ventures, including one with his wife Linda. In this case, new collaborative relationships provided a necessary separation that turned out to be permanent.

Hugo von Hofmannsthal and Richard Strauss had a collaboration that persisted for more than 25 years. The operas created by the poet and the composer in the early twentieth century were praised for their creativity both lyrically and musically. Over the course of this relationship (which ended when Hofmannsthal died) both men routinely collaborated with others. They also brought back ideas from these collaborations and from immersing themselves in the work of others.[8] These other relationships did, on occasion, stir feelings, mostly within Von Hofmannsthal who feared that the older, more famous of the two would find him lacking. Ultimately, these other collaborations did not threaten their continued work together. It is interesting to note that Hofmannsthal was quite willing and able to confess his insecurities to Strauss.

> I must confess that I was somewhat piqued by your scant and cool reception of the finished manuscript of *Ariadne* compared with the warm welcome you gave to every single act of *Rosenkavalier* – which stands out as one of the most significant pleasures connected with that work – and although we certainly agree in wishing to shun anything like the false show of mutual adulation in which mediocre artists indulge, I cannot help asking myself whether any praise in all the world could make up to me for the absence of yours.[9]

And Strauss regularly was willing and able to reassure him of his admiration for what Hofmannsthal brought to their joint work "In a collaboration like this I look upon you at the same time as my critic and my public."[10] Had Hofmannsthal not been as open as he was and Strauss not as reassuring, the insecurities might have grown making them harder to manage.

The importance of accepting and even welcoming separation in a collaboration cannot be overstated. Yet it is the least well-understood or managed characteristic of these relationships. Broaching the subject, often complicated by feelings of guilt or responsibility, and responding to a collaborator who has raised the issue can challenge any relationship. When the subject of spending time apart is brought up in a collaboration, it can be helpful to allow the intense feelings into the conversation. When the feelings, having been expressed have lessened, it may be possible to consider the possibility and benefits of separation, including how to decide together when and if the separation should end. A separation may last a few minutes, a few hours, days, weeks, or years, but it is always necessary for the vibrancy of the collaboration and the two people involved.

Endnotes

1 Sheila Lukins and Julee Rosso, *The New Basics Cookbook* (New York: Workman Publishing, 1989).
2 Miroslav Volf, *Exclusion and Embrace: A Theological Exploration of Identity, Otherness, and Reconciliation* (Nashville, TN: Abingdon Press, 1996).
3 Miroslav Volf, *Exclusion and Embrace: A Theological Exploration of Identity, Otherness, and Reconciliation* (Nashville, TN: Abingdon Press, 1996).
4 Personal interview.
5 Personal interview.
6 David Sheff and G. Barry Golson, *The Playboy Interviews with John Lennon and Yoko Ono* (New York: Berkley Books, 1981).
7 Paul McCartney and Paul Muldoon, *A Life in Lyrics*, Podcast (New York: Pushkin Industries, October 18, 2023).
8 Franz H. Bartsch, *Letters of Hugo von Hofmannsthal and Richard Strauss* (Princeton: Princeton University Press, 1991).
9 Franz H. Bartsch, *Letters of Hugo von Hofmannsthal and Richard Strauss* (Princeton: Princeton University Press, 1991).
10 Franz H. Bartsch, *Letters of Hugo von Hofmannsthal and Richard Strauss* (Princeton: Princeton University Press, 1991).

Chapter 11

Conclusion

As I bring this exploration of two-person collaboration to a close, let's return to the themes and ideas that have emerged throughout this book. Our focus has been not merely on defining collaboration as the act of two individuals working together, but on a deeper understanding of how creativity and productivity arise from the interplay of differences and the tension those differences create. In these pages, we've seen how collaborations, while often romanticized as a smooth merging of minds, are in fact also characterized by challenges and struggles, both personal and interpersonal. Far from being mere disruptions, these struggles are essential to the collaborative process. Collaboration, we've seen, is much more than simple cooperation or coordination – it is a creative act born out of differences, and managing those differences is what keeps the collaboration fruitful.

Collaboration: More Than Working Together

My working definition of collaboration is "a creative connection across difference." This definition moves beyond the common conception of collaboration as simply working together toward a shared goal. Collaboration is a *relationship* that fosters creativity – a relationship that involves risk, vulnerability, and mutual engagement. It is not simply about getting things done, nor is it about efficiency. It is an act of creation during which the contributions of two individuals merge to produce something neither could have done alone. The examples we've examined, from artistic partnerships like Gilbert and Sullivan to scientific collaborations such as Doudna and Charpentier, demonstrate that collaboration requires more than just shared effort. These pairs didn't just pool their skills; their creative output was born from the interplay of their differences – their unique approaches to their craft, their distinct experiences, and the complementary ways they viewed the world. This dynamic is central to understanding why collaborations can be both powerful and difficult.

DOI: 10.4324/9781032701998-11

The Latin root of the word collaboration carries an experiential history with it and reminds us that to collaborate is to labor together. The Latin root "*labi*," which implies slipping or falling, underscores the inherent struggle within collaboration, a process that involves both effort (labor) and risk (collapse). Collaboration is, by its very nature, hard work – physically, emotionally, and intellectually. It is work that requires us to constantly negotiate the space between individuality and connection and to find creative potential within that dynamically negotiated space.

Creativity Through Difference

Throughout this book, I have emphasized the dual nature of the differences that fuel collaboration. One set of differences originates in the personal style of the collaborator, the way they write or talk or organize or prepare. Without those differences, there might be no need for collaboration, because the product would simply be an extension of one individual's mind. Difference creates the conditions for creativity because it introduces new perspectives, skills, and approaches that challenge each person involved. We looked at the creative tension between Lennon and McCartney, for example. Much has been made of their different personalities and approaches to songwriting – Lennon's edgier, introspective style contrasted with McCartney's more melodic, pop-focused sensibility. Their collaboration was successful not because they smoothed over these differences, but because they found ways to use them as a source of creativity. It was in the tension between their approaches that some of their greatest songs were born. "We Can Work It Out" is not just a lyric from a Beatles song, it could be the credo that enabled Lennon and McCartney to create together.

The other sources of difference between collaborators stem from the groups to which they belong, the groups that raised them or taught them. Some of these influences began early in life, others were acquired later through education and professional training. The role of difference in collaboration extends beyond personality or creative style to the ways of seeing the world. Different perspectives born of different life experiences can be a rich source of creativity. But working with and across differences is not a simple process. Different life experiences bring with them different histories and different historical lessons. The groups to which each of us belongs carry views of other groups. Collaboration across groups therefore can involve misunderstandings, conflicts, and frustration. Navigating these tensions requires patience and a willingness to engage with the other person's perspective, even when doing so can be profoundly uncomfortable.

Connection: Vulnerability and Engagement

While difference is essential to collaboration, it must be balanced by connection. A successful collaboration requires a relationship built on the belief that when my limitations are on display you will not exploit them. This is the definition of trust. And for trust to exist in a relationship, this belief must be mutual. A trusting connection allows the collaborators to navigate their differences and turn them into a source of creativity rather than division. We described four other elements of a collaborative connection, all critical to working across differences: presence, expression, acceptance, and engagement. In its simplest terms, a collaborative connection is one in which we can bring our differences to the work without fear of being rejected or ignored. In any collaborative relationship, there will be moments of uncertainty, where one person's vision or idea challenges the other's understanding. A trusting connection encourages the collaborators to share their ideas, even when they're not fully formed or when they diverge from the other's perspective. When these ideas are shared, a trusting connection is characterized by a joint willingness to engage these ideas. This trust is built over time as two individuals become increasingly secure in the belief that they will neither dismiss nor ignore each other's contributions.

The trust found in a collaboration points to my observation that collaboration is an intimate act. Sharing creative work with another person – especially when that work is still in progress – requires exposing oneself, one's thoughts and feelings, to another person. The more we can expose, the more material we generate for the collaboration. The vulnerability that comes with this exposure, with the possibility of rejection or judgment, is a necessary part of the collaborative process because it opens the door to true engagement. When both collaborators are willing to be vulnerable, to share their insecurities and uncertainties, they demonstrate their need for each other. What each person lacks they must depend on the other (or some outside contribution) to provide. Hiding, or trying to hide, my vulnerabilities from my collaborator while second nature to many of us, merely robs the collaboration of the potential represented by complementarity.

Coming Together and Falling Apart

An intimate connection, however, is not static. Just as differences can drive the creative process, they can also create tensions that threaten a relationship. Over time, the very factors that once drew collaborators together can begin to push them apart. This too is a natural part of the collaborative process, something that we must understand and manage if we are to sustain long-term creative partnerships.

One of the key observations of this book is that collaboration is not a steady, linear process. Collaborations tend to follow a cyclical pattern of coming together, falling apart, and coming together again. This ebb and flow is an essential part of the creative process, and understanding it is crucial for sustaining a collaboration. In the beginning stages of a collaboration, there is often a sense of excitement and possibility. This is the "falling together" phase, where the differences between collaborators feel fresh and energizing. Simultaneously, we tend to notice commonalities when relationships are forming. The creative possibilities dominate our images of the future. As the collaboration progresses, those same differences can begin to create friction. We begin to experience friction points that we did not notice at the outset. What once felt like a productive tension may start to feel like a source of irritation or conflict. It can also be true that the success of the collaboration heightens the tensions within the relationship concerning credit and acknowledgment. The world in which most collaborations are embedded often fails to see creativity in a *relationship*, rewarding one or the other collaborator to isolate the true source of the creative product. These external pressures on a collaborative relationship can further exacerbate tension between the two people.

But these moments of tension are not necessarily a sign that the collaboration is failing. In fact, they are often a sign that either the relationship itself needs attention because the differences that fuel creativity are now pushing the collaborators apart or the pressures of the outside world need to be managed by the collaborators lest these pressures pull the relationship apart. The tensions that arise are a natural part of the collaborative process, and they offer an opportunity for growth and reinvention. The challenge is to find ways to navigate these tensions without letting them destroy the relationship. Most often this navigation process involves the two collaborators facing the issues and emotions together.

The Necessity of Separation

Sometimes navigating the tensions in a collaboration, both the ones that originate within the collaborative relationship as well as the ones that originate outside it, involves getting out – stepping away from the relationship. This idea may seem counterintuitive, especially in a culture that often views separation as a sign of failure. It seems paradoxical. How can we create together when we are apart? But as we've seen throughout this book, collaboration is not about permanent fusion, the collapse of two individuals into one collaborative entity. It is about the creative tension that comes from maintaining both connection and individuality. And sometimes, the best way to preserve that balance is to step away.

Separation allows collaborators to reconnect with their own identities, to return to the environments that nourish their individual creativity, and to bring fresh perspectives back to the partnership. This is not a rejection of the collaboration but a necessary part of sustaining it. By stepping away, collaborators can prevent the relationship from becoming stale or one-sided, and they can ensure that the differences that fuel creativity remain intact. Coming together, falling apart, and coming together again mirrors the natural rhythms of creativity itself. Creativity is not a constant, uninterrupted process – it involves periods of rest, reflection, and renewal. Collaboration too embodies these cycles.

The Whole Story

One of the most important takeaways from this book is the need to tell the whole story of collaboration. Too often, we focus only on the positive aspects of collaboration – the moments of creative synergy, the successful outcomes, and the harmony of working together. But as we've seen, collaboration is more complex than that. It involves struggle, conflict, and moments of doubt. It requires constant negotiation between individuality and connection, between difference and commonality. By telling the whole story, not only the good parts, we can better prepare ourselves for the realities of collaboration. We can learn to see moments of tension not as failures but as opportunities for growth. We can recognize that separation is a natural part of the process that can strengthen the collaboration in the long run. And we can understand that collaboration, like any relationship, requires each person to confront their own demons, their own limitations if there is to exist the possibility of creativity emerging from a relationship. Complementarity is one of the cornerstones of a collaborative connection. As we have noted, repeatedly, complementarity rests on each of us developing an accepting relationship with our shortcomings. Only by doing this can we accept the contributions of a collaborator.

In the spirit of telling the whole story, I want to address a question that has been posed to me ever since I undertook the writing of this book. Isn't it ironic that a person with several meaningful collaborations chose to write a book about this topic alone? Why did I do this? The answers to this question are embedded in the exploration of collaboration in the preceding pages.

Most of my early professional career was marked by satisfying and productive collaborations in the areas of academic writing and teaching as well as academic administration. My first published paper was a three-person collaboration. My first book was a two-person collaboration. I loved the intensity that working with someone (as opposed to working alone) involves. Most startling to me was the fact that I thought differently in a relationship than I did at home in the privacy of my own thoughts. My collaborator's ideas and reactions literally propelled my own thinking in totally new directions. And this process seemed to be mutual. It was not unusual for me to finish a project and sit in awe at what we had created out of our relationship. I also noticed that these collaborations were not always smooth sailing, but my real appreciation for the challenges in collaboration came later.

Around the time that my second and third book projects,[1,2] both collaborations with Smith, were coming to an end, I was also deeply involved in an administrative collaboration at my academic institution with Clayton Alderfer, a former teacher who had evolved into a trusted friend and colleague. Both collaborations had all the elements described in this book. As psychologists, we were all committed to examining ourselves and our relationships (complete with our respective blind spots and defenses). The work was satisfying, and the relationships were intimate, intense, and supportive. But there was a voice in my head, speaking softly most of the time, but quite persistent. The voice kept asking if my contribution to these collaborations made a difference. The voice kept questioning what I brought to these relationships.

Through the lenses of this book, one could say that the voice was the manifestation of my insecurities and limitations, insecurities highlighted by my perception of the strengths of my collaborators and my own limitations not yet "acceptable" to me. As the years went by, I wrote and taught on my own but had trouble shaking the feeling that I was leaching off my collaborations, borrowing ideas that were co-created but not equitably so. The more I involved myself in collaborations with Smith, Alderfer, and others, the more I experienced the satisfaction of relational creativity *and* the more the question of my own identity kept being posed to me by this internal voice. The more I worked alone, the more I confronted my limitations and the more I missed the satisfactions of collaboration. When I wrote alone, it often felt like I was making lists. The feeling drove me toward collaboration. But when I worked with someone, I questioned my own contribution and this feeling drove me to individual work, work that might quiet my internal doubts.

Over time, as I got older and my individual identity became more recognizable both to me and to the world around me, my professional path diverged from that of my closest collaborators. We were not at the same institution which made it easier to diverge. When I confronted, examined, and accepted the events and feelings described in this book, especially in my enduring relationship with Smith, I began to hear another internal voice. Midwifed by years of psychotherapy, what emerged was an internal conversation about who I was alone and who I was in collaboration. I began to accept that collaborations were my preferred way of being in the world *and* that I wanted to explore what comes from my alone time as well. This realization struck me as a classic illustration of the Jungian contention that our persona and our shadow are always both with us struggling to be integrated.

In the years leading up to this book, I chose more individual writing and teaching projects to go along with my collaborative work. These efforts became more and more satisfying (though never easy). I felt myself developing a muscle that I had long neglected, favoring instead ones that felt more comfortable and responsive. Making these choices meant turning down some collaborations, most notably, but not surprisingly with Alderfer and Smith, both of whom regularly pitched a writing project to me. I feared getting lost in the collaboration this time, just as I was beginning to invest in my individual-ness. Both collaborators evolved with me, supporting the individual work, and tugging only gently and lovingly at the collaborative strings that connected us.

Still, my initial thoughts about a personal writing project did not involve the topic of collaboration. I wanted to write about relationships being at the core of everything that happens in organizations. The working title of this imagined book was "It's All About Relationships." But I couldn't get out of the starting block. Since at this point in my professional life, the only reason to write anything was because I wanted to, apparently, I did not want to write about relationships. One day, as I was cleaning out file cabinets, I came upon a folder on collaboration. It contained notes from the late 1980s and the transcript of a colloquium Catherine Durnell Crampton and I had given in 1987. I was intrigued by the notes, reading them with growing interest. For me, the decades between 1987 and 2020 have been filled with collaboration. I found myself drawn to a writing project that would convey what I had learned about collaboration in the hopes that my experience would inform, in a supportive way, the experience of others.

I believe the reason I chose to make this book an individual project is because I needed time apart from my collaborations to explore my individual-ness. I have been enriched by my collaborations and learned a great deal about myself and about collaborative relationships. This moment in my life felt like the time to give *individual* expression to that learning, ironically about collaboration. Collaborations never left my life during the period of my individual work, but I can feel the urge to return to them with enthusiasm as this book nears completion.

Collaboration

In closing, this book has sought to provide a deeper understanding of two-person collaboration – a complex, dynamic relationship that fosters creativity through difference. Collaboration is a journey that involves both coming together and falling apart, both connection and separation. It is a process that requires trust, vulnerability, and a willingness to engage both the other's perspective and one's own shadow, two often quite daunting challenges. Even when collaborations don't last, they leave behind a legacy, a creative product as well as insight into the collaborative process. The first can be easy to see. The second reveals itself as we inquire into the dynamics of the collaborative relationship. This inquiry can teach us much about the relational aspects of creativity. If we can bring these relational dimensions of all collaborations out of the shadows, what we see has the potential for enriching and sustaining our collaborations.

Endnotes

1 David N. Berg and Kenwyn K. Smith, *Paradoxes of Group Life: Understanding Conflict, Paralysis, and Movement in Group Dynamics* (San Francisco, CA: Jossey-Bass, 1987).

2 David N. Berg and Kenwyn K. Smith, *The Self in Social Inquiry: Researching Methods* (Beverly Hills: Sage Publications, 1988).

Index

Printed in the United States
by Baker & Taylor Publisher Services